EXPERT PROFILES
VOLUME 10

Conversations with Influencers & Innovators

EXPERT PROFILES
VOLUME 10

Conversations with Influencers & Innovators

Sarah Outlaw

Simon Skipper

Richard Fletcher

Henry Johnstone

John Marshall

Ruth Nicholson

Monique Breault

Debora Masten

Nicole Tennison

Royalties from the Retail Sales of "Expert Profiles" are donated to Global Autism Project

AUTISM KNOWS **NO BORDERS;**
FORTUNATELY NEITHER DO WE.®

Global Autism Project 501(c)3, is a nonprofit organization which provides training to local individuals in evidence-based practices for individuals with autism.

Global Autism Project believes that every child has the ability to learn and their potential should not be limited by geographical bounds.

The Global Autism Project seeks to eliminate the disparity in service provision seen around the world by providing high-quality training to individuals providing services in their local community. This training is made sustainable through regular training trips and contiguous remote training.

You can learn more about Global Autism Project by visiting GlobalAutismProject.org.

Table of Contents

Sarah Outlaw – How Nutrition Response Testing is
Helping Children and Families With Unique
Nutrition Programs to Transform Their Health 1

Simon Skipper – Transform Into Your Next-Level
Self 19

Richard Fletcher – How to Effectively Promote
Yourself on Facebook 35

Henry Johnstone – Access Your King's Energy 57

John Marshall – How to Create a Framework for
Success as a Small Business Owner 75

Ruth Nicholson – Key Concepts For Productive &
Efficient Meetings 85

Monique Breault – How To Maximize Your
Potential & Gain Confidence Through
Leadership Development & Coaching 97

Debora Masten – The Importance of Advanced
Training for Spa Profitability 111

Nicole Tennison – Mistakes to Avoid When
Getting A First Time Home Loan 121

How Nutrition Response Testing is Helping Children and Families With Unique Nutrition Programs to Transform Their Health

Sarah Outlaw, MH, MSACN is the Owner, Lead Practitioner and Director of Natural Health Improvement Center of South Jersey and Natural Health Improvement Center of Des Moines. She holds a Master's Degree in Applied Clinical Nutrition from New York Chiropractic College, and has earned professional certificates as a Health Coach, Clinical Herbalist, and Advanced Nutrition Response Testing® Practitioner.

She is the author and publisher of the Real Food Outlaws blog, where she writes about real food, natural living, and holistic health. Her mission and purpose are to help get sick people well without the use of drugs or surgery and to teach other practitioners to do the same.

Conversation with Sarah Outlaw

Tell us about Natural Health Improvement Centers and how you are helping your patients.

Sarah Outlaw: We are not your typical Nutritionists here at Natural Health Improvement Centers of South Jersey and Des Moines. What we do is very specific. A traditional Nutritionist will just take a symptom survey or get an intake form and then give you nutritional advice and maybe give supplements based on your symptoms. Or, if they are a Functional Nutritionist, they might order some blood work, have stool samples ordered, or do more Functional Medicine type tests. We do a form of kinesiology known as "Nutrition Response Testing®" developed by Dr. Freddie Ulan, founder of Ulan Nutritional Systems, INC to actually get to the root cause of what you have going, give you an assessment of what's going on in your body, specifically find what nutrition you're deficient in, and exactly what nutrition you need at that time.

How does the Central Nervous System impact responses in their body?

Sarah Outlaw: I'll backtrack a little bit and give you a definition of Nutrition Response Testing®. It is a non-invasive way of testing the body for food sensitivities, immune system challenges, metals, chemicals, molds, environmental toxins, etc.

We specifically use the muscle strength of the body to test the nervous system. We are specifically testing the

Autonomic Nervous System. So, when we think of the nervous system, usually people will think of chiropractic spinal adjustments that correct the nervous system. Well, think a little bit deeper into the cellular structure of the body, what makes the body run, and look at the Autonomic Nervous System.

A simple explanation of this that I use with all of my patients is that the Autonomic Nervous System is the part of the nervous system that does all the things that you don't have to think about doing on a daily basis, such making your eyes blink, or your heart beat, or your lungs breathe. There are two main parts to this that we test. We test the sympathetic part of the nervous system, which is in charge of all the active things your body does, including movement, your heart rate, blood pressure, respiration, stress response, all those action type things.

We also test another part, and this is really important because a lot of our patients come in with some of these issues that this part is in charge of. The parasympathetic part of the nervous system is in charge of resting, digesting, and healing. People come in and see us and are not able to sleep, they're not able to digest their food, or they're having stomach issues. Why this is so important is because these two parts of the Autonomic Nervous System run on nutrition, which is why we are so concerned about it.

We do the testing to find out why these two parts are not working well together. Is your nutrition not right for you? Or, are you not absorbing what you're eating? We get to the root cause of your symptoms and find out what's going on. We want to know what's going on in this system specifically, which is what makes us so unique.

Do you work with chiropractors as well because it seems like that would be a good synergistic relationship?

Sarah Outlaw: Yes, we do, and what I do is sometimes known as "Chiropractic Nutrition" because it was started by chiropractors who were doing adjustments, and they weren't holding. They found that there was actually a nutritional component in their patients and if they corrected the nutrition, the chiropractic adjustments would hold and they wouldn't have the same muscular/skeletal issues week after week, month after month. That is how this started with kinesiology decades ago.

What are the advantages of unique individual nutrition programs that help you transform the health for children and families experiencing a variety of health problems?

Sarah Outlaw: We really want to get to the children. That's our ultimate goal because we can stop many of the issues that are plaguing our kids like ADD, ADHD, digestive issues, asthma, allergies, eczema. If we can get to the kids and correct their health now, their futures will be much brighter! They're healthier as they go through school, as they get older, and they won't have as many fertility issues, mental health issues, autoimmune disease, etc. We get mom or dad on a nutrition program first to get them started on the process of getting healthy; seeing how this works. And then we either at the same time or shortly after mom or dad come in, we get the children on a natural health with us as well.

As a family, they are working together, changing and improving their food, taking whole foods, supplements, sometimes some herbal supplements, maybe some homeopathic remedies to get their bodies back under management, and we go from there. We do a lot of education as well because we want to teach them how to fish so to speak when it comes to healthy eating and nutrition, not just throw them some fish.

We teach them how to eat, how to feed their children, what good food and good healthy eating means. We have hundreds and hundreds of kids on a program already in both of our practices and they are doing incredible. This is very encouraging to us!

What do you feel are the biggest myths out there when it comes to unique individual nutrition programs?

Sarah Outlaw: The main thing I find that they have misconceptions about is that we are going to take away all the food that they love. They think, "Okay, she's just going to take everything I eat away and do a bulk elimination." But that's not what we do. We specifically find the exact things your body is sensitive to, what's causing inflammation, and then just do a temporary elimination of those while we're fixing the immune system and the digestive system.

Usually those foods that were eliminated can be added back in, but in the meantime, we're teaching them how to eat healthy so they won't want to add in the ice cream, or the pizza, or the pasta all the time. We completely change their mindset and in reality, their whole health paradigm.

People also will come in and they think that since we use nutritional supplements, they can bring in whatever vitamins that they currently use and those will be enough. But that's not the case because most supplements or vitamins on the market are actually synthetic. They're nutraceutical which basically means "vitamin pharmaceutical." You are getting pieces of different vitamins in chemical form that are artificially "vitaminizing" your body, so to speak, instead of nourishing your body. You are not getting nutrition; you're just getting synthetic forms of vitamins.

We use several different product lines and we test them, and they were also tested by the school that I attended. We use mainly Standard Process and MediHerb because of the quality. Standard Process is all whole food, and MediHerb is very pure, therapeutic herbs. I know what I'm giving, what I'm testing, and I know it's going to be quality. I know that there are no adulterations. I know that there are no counterfeits. I know that they are fresh, and I know that they not coming third party because who knows what's in those bottles ordered online!

We do very, very specific targeted nutrition, which is exactly what you need. If someone brings in their own vitamins, I'll test them. Sometimes they test okay. Sometimes they don't. We do muscle testing, but we really want to focus on the quality and the importance of whole food nutrition, not synthetics.

What are some of the most common fears your patients have when they come in?

Sarah Outlaw: We try to dispel their fears by addressing them at their "report of findings" visit where they get all their test results and we tell them about their program so they want to know what they're going to be doing for the next six or more months. People are mostly afraid of having to eliminate foods. They also fear reactions and don't want to feel sick and have withdrawal symptoms from eliminating sugar. They don't want to have Herxheimer reactions, which can be like a withdrawal or a repeat of old symptoms coming back.

They don't want to have those healing crises. We explain what could possibly happen in the beginning of the protocol. We do things very specifically in our program so that they avoid those symptoms. We use a lot of what we call "lymphatic drainage" which works to keep the liver clear. We're keeping the lymphatic system clear, and all of the body's exit channels open so that they don't have things building up in their system and get sick. Most of the time when people come in, they do not have any reactions. But we warn them, we give them worst case scenario to dispel those fears and say, "Hey, you're probably not going to have this happen, but if you do, just give the office a call."

So, the first fear is having to eliminate foods. The second one is a possible healing "reaction."

The third thing is being able to stick to a program. We do short increments that we call "healing cycles." A healing cycle for the body is about four months. That's about how long it takes for the red blood cells to replace themselves in the body. So, we call that a healing cycle. We do our protocol for four months, so people commit to four months—one healing cycle. We do a reevaluation at that time, and then we go from there.

Most people need another healing cycle, but by that time, they're feeling so good and they're doing so well that they can't wait to do another one to see how much more their body can heal itself. So, we go step-by-step making sure that whatever concerns and fears they do have, we keep the lines of communication open. We are taking care of them right away so that people are completely comfortable with their program with us.

What are some mistakes that people make during these healing cycles?

Sarah Outlaw: Most of the time we see that people don't start feeling better right away because, for example, they're used to having a headache and taking Ibuprofen or Tylenol and feeling better in 15 minutes. So, we always explain that it's not a quick fix and it's not emergency room care, but it is a long-term sustainable change to get your body where you need to be and allow you to reach optimal health. But it takes time.

We know what all the objections are going to be and all the obstacles that people are going to run into. So, we try to dispel them in the beginning to coach them through… you can call me and my Associate Practitioners Health Coaches if you would like, and we'll coach you through!

We also see a lot of people feeling better very quickly and then not wanting to follow through with the rest of their healing cycle. So, "Oh my gosh, you gave me these herbs. I feel great now." Or, "My skin looks so great, I'm good. Okay, bye."

You can't do that. Symptoms are subjective – your body's not done healing!

The herbs that we use are so powerful and they do work like a medicine almost, nourishing the body and healing, so you can get a quick response to those. But we must do some foundational work to get those organs to be able to function at optimum, and to get your body to what we call a new homeostasis or a new level of health.

We really must keep you on a protocol.

Even after that four-to-six months, or even eight months, is over, we have people who are on maintenance with us and they come in every one, three, six or 12 months, or as needed to continue a preventative health care program with us. So, we're monitoring them and keeping them healthy for the rest of their lives!

It is important to understand because healing takes time. I also like to say is that healing is not linear, so you are going to feel better and then not feel better because things happen. You might get the flu, you might get sick with a cold, or you might get a stomach bug. Things are going to happen that are going to delay your healing process and that doesn't mean you're failing, but you must understand that this is a process and trust the process. Always keep moving forward. I start to get really cliché when it comes to these things but it's the truth: "Keep moving forward and keep the momentum."

The healing is not linear concept is so important because we don't want people to get discouraged. My own healing was not short. It took eme years to recover from things that I had. I had Lyme disease, I had hypo-thyroid, adrenal fatigue. I had multiple miscarriages and horrible skin acne.

My associate practitioners are the same way. So, our patients look at us and think, "Okay, you guys are all really healthy and you look great now." But it took us a long time to get here.

We do our program on a very gradual scale, so clients can expect moving forward to get to that new level of health. If they go back to eating the way they used to eat (pizza, hoagies, etc.), of course their bodies are going to become inflamed again or respond negatively because they're reintroducing an inflammatory food. It doesn't mean that their body slid backwards. They can maintain the level of health they achieved on a natural health improvement program continuing a healthy way of eating.

This doesn't mean they can't have that hoagie or sub occasionally, or that piece of pizza, or that piece of cake on their birthday. Their body will be able to handle it at some point because once healing happens, the body can manage inflammation better. Their digestive system is healed, so they can digest things better. They might feel like they are more sensitive to those foods that they are eliminating in the first one or two healing cycles, but after a while there'll be able to eat those in moderation again. There will be what we call a "threshold" where they'll know, their body will tell them if they had too many cookies or too much pizza because they'll start to feel not well.

People say to me all the time, "I didn't know how bad I felt until I didn't feel bad anymore." So, they feel really,

really good, and then they'll eat something and say, "Wow, this is how I used to feel, and guess what? This is what caused it. That cookie caused me to feel bad 10 years ago."

They start to make the connections.

I don't have to say anything because their bodies are telling them exactly what's happening. It's the coolest thing because a lot of times as a person of authority in the nutrition field, people think, "Oh, I don't want to listen to her. She's going to tell me what to eat."

But if their body's telling them, and they feel it, and they see it, and other people notice, it makes a huge difference in their health!

Can you share an example of how you have helped a patient overcome these obstacles and succeed?

Sarah Outlaw: Sure! We had a patient recently. She's a young mom and she had recently experienced some pretty severe skin rashes and it was depressing her. She came in and she was extremely upset because her doctors told her they didn't know what was wrong. They couldn't figure out the source of these hives and rashes that would randomly come and go. Under her arms she had rashes, eczema, was very itchy, she would get bumps all over her face; and it was kind of embarrassing for her. She's well known in the community and she has little kids and was always out and about.

She came to me desperate and in tears needing help.

She's been on our program for six weeks, and she came in yesterday for her six-week checkup. And I asked her how she was feeling, and a huge smile came on her face, and she said, "Sarah, I feel great. And, I just went on vacation and I'm feeling amazing." She lifted her arms and there was no rash. Her skin looks beautiful. She was one of those people who said, "I'm going to do whatever you tell me because I can't live like this anymore. These rashes, I just want to scratch my skin off."

It was so bad. She would be up all night scratching, and we found some underlying immune system issues causing this.

We tested for things like parasites, bacteria, fungus, yeast, viruses. We can't diagnose because we're not MDs, but we can test for categories of immune system issues. A lot of times with these skin issues, we find parasites and fungus together. Once we handle those microorganism issues and get the gut rebalanced, it is amazing how quickly these skin issues can resolve themselves. This had been going on for over a year for her, and she was just desperate.

What inspired you to become a Nutrition Response Testing Practitioner?

Sarah Outlaw: My own health. I lived in California a few years back and I was just getting into the holistic lifestyle with my children. I was a new mom and I started a Holistic Moms Network Chapter in my local town of Santa Clarita, California. One of the presenters was a Nutrition Response Testing® Practitioner. I had never heard of it before. She bought test kits with her with these little vials that have all the testers in them with some supplements. And she asked, "Who wants to volunteer?" And I said, "I'll volunteer." So, she tested me, and she said,

"Listen, I see that you have acne. It looks like you have some fatigue and stress issues, why don't you come and see me?"

So, I started to see her and continued for about three months and then we moved back to New Jersey where I live now. But there wasn't anyone near me who does Nutrition Response® Testing. I was at a loss, so I started my education in herbal medicine. I was also getting some health coaching and herbal certifications. I had just had my fourth baby and my chiropractor at that time asked me if I was interested in doing some nutritional consulting in his office. And I said, "Yes, but I need to be able to have a little bit more under my belt as far as how am I going to test these people because I don't have any ability to get blood work done." At that point, I was only a health coach. So, I started my education in Nutrition Response Testing® and I was able to start a practice with him, and then went out on my own after about a year.

I've been practicing in New Jersey, and this is my fifth year, my fourth year in private practice. A year and a half ago I was asked by a friend and colleague to open a practice in Iowa, so we did that, and it has been one of the fastest growing practices in the country! And it was all because of my own struggles with my health!

My grandmother died at 40 of cancer. I never got to meet her. I'm 40 now, so she was dead at my age. And all my grandparents have passed away from different types of cancer. These are things that I don't want in my family. I'm trying to change that with my own children and make sure that myself, my husband, my children, and my family are healthy.

I'm also committed to giving that to everyone else around me in my communities; my Iowa community, New Jersey community and around the country teaching what I do to other Practitioners. It is from our own experiences that we can best help other people.

What's the most important question someone experiencing a variety of health problems should ask themselves as they consider individual nutrition programs?

Sarah Outlaw: They must understand that Nutrition Response Testing® is different than anything that they've ever experienced; they have to keep an open mind and understand that because it's biochemistry and physics, a lot of people don't understand it right away. There's a lot that goes into it. We're actually communicating with what we call the "innate intelligence" of the body and to the "naked eye" or to our sometimes closed minds, that doesn't seem possible. You must think of it like biofeedback that you're not using a machine for. We are using our hands as the machine for the muscle response. Our process is so good and we want you to understand it because we want you to feel really comfortable when you come to see us and know that you're going to be able to get help.

I could have 10 people come in today, new patients with the exact same symptoms. I would tell them, "You can have the same symptoms as the 10 other people in the room, but your test results and your nutrition and food protocols will be completely different." No two people are ever the same because your individual needs are different. The root cause of your symptoms is different, so a targeted, so it is important you have an individualized Nutrition Response Testing® and Designed Clinical Nutrition Program. This really is what draws people in and gets them to realize that we are different. We can help you and that you can find what you're looking for here at our office.

What's the most important thing someone should consider when evaluating a Nutrition Response Testing Practitioner?

Sarah Outlaw: Nutrition Response Testing Practitioners have gone through all the Advanced Clinical Training at Ulan Nutritional Systems, Inc. in Florida. We're all trained the same, so you can expect to get the same care as you would get from myself or my Associate Practitioners. We refer clients to each other quite often, which is great.

One thing that sets us apart, and people always ask me, "Why do you sell supplements if I could just go down the street and buy vitamins?" We touched on this a little bit earlier, but the supplements are what we call "nutritional therapy", food as medicine. We're looking to provide you with the genuine replacement parts your body needs to fix the underlying issues you have going on! You need something to make the corrections to the Autonomic Nervous System while the body is healing itself. Whole food supplements along with healthy food is how we accomplish that. You have to do both: food and whole food supplements.

I went to a Naturopathic Doctor a few years ago when I was really, really sick after the birth of my fourth baby.

My system completely crashed. I was charged $450 to walk through her door and $250 for every follow-up visit. And every time I would go, she would just give me supplements without testing and say, "Try these and see how they work for you." Well, they didn't work. So, $10,000 later, I felt just as bad as I did when I first walked through the door in the first place! I said, "There has to be a better way. There must be a better way than this. I have to find that better way and give that to people."

So that was one thing that catapulted me into being able to provide this service for my community.

How can someone find out more about Sarah Outlaw and Natural Health Improvement Centers and how you can help?

Sarah Outlaw: The best way is just to start out on our websites (New Jersey – www.nhicsouthjersey.com and Des Moines – www.nhicdesmoines.com).

You can find us on Facebook and Instagram. We post a lot and I do a lot of live videos. We broadcast all our workshops live that we do in-house. You can get a lot of information that way.

If you are not in Iowa or in New Jersey, you can find a clinician who does what we do by going to the Ulan Nutritional Systems website at www.unsinc.info. There's a clinician finder on the site that will help you find a clinician close to you to get the care that you need.

About Sarah Outlaw and Natural Health Improvement Centers of South Jersey and Des Moines

Offering safe, natural solutions for many health problems from newborn babies all the way through 80+ years of age, Natural Health Improvement Centers of South Jersey and Des Moines is helping many people find a natural, non-invasive way to improve their health. They practice "Root Cause Nutrition." Symptoms are present because there is something going on in the body that needs to be found and handled. They help their clients eliminate the root cause of their health issues to be well and thrive.

Contact Sarah

For more information on either of the Natural Health Improvement Centers in either Iowa or New Jersey:

EMAIL
info@nhicdesmoines.com or
info@nhicsouthjersey.com

FACEBOOK
Facebook.com/NHICSouthJersey
Facebook.com/NHICDesMoines

INSTAGRAM
Instagram.com/NHICSouthJersey
Instagram.com/NHICDesMoines

Transform Into
Your Next-Level Self

Simon Skipper Christiansen is a transformational photographer and a dynamic and courageous adventurer. The stories of his life are as varied as they are astounding. During the time spent walking on (and skateboarding across) the planet, Simon has experienced a dizzying array of situations that have shaped him into who he is today; a person intent on sharing his insight with others so that they can finally step into the hiking boots they were born to wear and carve out a path to their future.

He is here today to talk about how to transform into your next-level self which will enable you to become the person you need to be, to be able to hit your goals!

Conversation with Simon Skipper

Welcome, Simon. It's a real pleasure to talk to you today. Your photography is incredible!

Simon Skipper: Thanks! It's a pleasure to be here.

Can you define exactly what it means to be a transformational photographer and explain how that differs from a regular photographer?

Simon Skipper: It's a term that came to mind when I was reflecting on my business. When I work with my clients I use all these different skills; therapeutic skills, coaching, and people skills. Stepping out into the spotlight can be really daunting unless you're used it, and by using my skills, I help people to access the truest version of themselves and then we bring that across in their images.

I wanted to help people to stand out by being courageous and to drop the façade that we all carry around. I had feedback from numerous clients telling me that they got so much more out of working with me than only a bunch of nice photographs. They told me they felt like they had been through a transformation… and the term transformational photographer was born!

I had a look at your photography, and I have to say that every photo tells a story. For the people out there who want to transform into their next-level self, what is the first thing they need to do?

Simon Skipper: The first thing is they have to do is change their focus. There is a story where if you're driving down a desert road, you crash into a lamppost, but it's the only lamppost around for miles, and every year about forty cars crash into it. There could be one post every one hundred and fifty miles, but because it's the only thing around, it draws your focus, and what you're looking at is where you're heading.

If you only keep looking at the problem, you're not going to solve it. You have to acknowledge yourself and know that your emotions work; your guidance system works, the inner GPS as I like to call it, and it's telling you, "I'm not where I'm supposed to be." It's important for us to base our decisions on our values without compromise. Contrast is actually a great thing. It might not feel like it at the time but imagine if we didn't have that navigation system. We'd be completely lost.

So, they need to shift their focus off the problem, or what they don't want and onto...

Simon Skipper: The solution and what they DO want.

This is definitely something I notice a lot in people.

Simon Skipper: Exactly. "I don't want to be broke!" "I don't want to be treated like dirt!" and "I don't want to live in this place!" are all examples of people focusing on the problem. Unconscious brain forces often get in the way of delayed gratification, for example, someone who is financially troubled reaffirming to herself 'the money is always gone at the end of the month anyway, so I might as well have that relatively expensive burger.'

So, the more they try to get away from that problem, the more of the same they are attracting. Let's say they crack that. What's next?

Simon Skipper: Next, we have to find a strategy. We could ask somebody, "What sort of person do you want a relationship with?" and they could say, "They shouldn't be fat, and they shouldn't smoke," but that's not answering the question. Ask yourself what you do want, don't focus on the limitations.

Remember to feel into your heart when setting goals and creating your strategy. Dare to follow your heart unapologetically, even when it's hard, and your fulfilment has to come.

You'll know that you're aligned by asking yourself, "Is this goal/person/activity aligned with who I truly am and where I'm going?" The repercussions of not following your heart will be an inner emptiness that no stimulant can fill. Have the courage to live your truth.

When it comes to transformation, you have to tell yourself, and your friends, what you do want, not what isn't working. "I want a kind man who I can love, and we can grow old together. Not to be dependent on each other, but really grow together and experience life together."

Write it down. That's so powerful. You can write down a little guidance note, or love letter; your Ten Commandments almost. That's what I do. Sometimes I ask myself "What's my ideal outcome in a world where everything is possible?" Then I write it down. You have to make it realistic though. It's not something I do a hundred times a week. But as long as you're going in the right direction, circumstances are going to unfold.

Again, if we're driving along a road from Paris to Amsterdam, we don't want to complain that we're not there yet. So, the first step is to acknowledge to yourself that you want to change and resolve to make that change, and then write it down.

Step one is to change the focus, step two is finding a strategy, what's step three?

Simon Skipper: The third step is to share, get some leverage. We can tell ourselves, for example, that our job isn't so bad, but why do this when there are thousands of jobs out there where we could bring our skills and talents? We're robbing ourselves of quality of life and value when we settle.

I 'll share a great little anecdote because I am a great believer in leverage. Les Brown, a motivational speaker, was sharing this story of a man who was hearing strange sounds coming from his neighbour's house. When he asked the man what the howling and squeaks were, the neighbour told him that his dog was sitting on a nail. When asked why the dog didn't move, he was told that it didn't hurt enough yet. So you can ask yourself, "What sort of nails do I have in my life that don't hurt enough?" And then decide not to tolerate them anymore.

That's the danger zone isn't it? When we're at rock bottom, we know we have to change. But when we're in our comfort zone, it's harder to change. Do you agree?

Simon Skipper: Exactly, that's what I mean. Stop tolerating these things we're "supposed" to tolerate. And start asking for support. Get coaching, or an accountability buddy; someone who will help keep you on track. Someone who will remind you of why it's so important to you.

I love that! Just to rewind a little, you were talking about strategy. You mentioned something called the Ten Commandments. Can you tell us about that?

Simon Skipper: It doesn't have to absolutely be ten, but I'm a big believer in positive self-talk.

There has been a big trend within the personal growth sector of affirmations. I'm not necessarily against affirmations, but they're not taking us the whole way there. Unfortunately, Law of Attraction contains a lot of pseudoscience. If you feel you're ugly and fat, standing in front of a mirror and telling yourself that you are pretty and slim isn't going to work because your subconscious knows that isn't the truth. It's not enough to know something intellectually. You have to also be there emotionally, consider your challenges and take massive action.

Things have to be believable for yourself, so instead of standing there saying, "I'm a millionaire", because there is also a lot of talk about financial freedom, tell yourself that you are getting better and better at attracting money every day. Tell yourself that you are looking at opportunities to gain wealth and love, whatever your focus is, and that you are finding them. "I'm gravitating naturally to the things that I know in my heart I want." "I'm opening myself up to sources and positive surprises and I can't even know where they come from." Just go on a rampage!

One of my greatest teachers is Abraham/Esther Hicks. Their story really caught my eye when I discovered it. Abraham is a conscious entity that is channeled through a woman called Esther Hicks, and 'he' gives her blocks of understanding. They do a lot of this positive energy work. Because emotional suffering is not a good perspective from which to start your goal-setting and strategy.

Great! And where does the photography fit into this transformational experience?

Simon Skipper: It's a fact that 90% of the information we interpret in our lives is done by our visual perception. That means your perception of yourself and surroundings. Anything that matters to you is hugely important. What I'm able to do is combine my insights, work in personal growth, and visualisation with my photography to create these visualisations, "Make your life your own movie." Or create a portrait of you as a person you see yourself as. Or, for your organisation to really stand out and get to the core or soul of the direction you want to go that's really pushing you and tailoring the story exactly to your needs. It can also be combined with coaching and strategy.

I've never heard anything like this before, the combination of coaching and photography. It's fantastic. I've been reading up a lot about you, Simon. You're a photographer and life coach; you've had so many adventures.

Simon Skipper: That's what life is about.

I have to ask. What happened in Hawaii?

Simon Skipper: I decided to travel for a year after high school because I needed to find myself. I'd never travelled much with my family, especially not to exotic locations. So, I travelled for a year, and one place I went to was Hawaii to visit a family friend. It was very chilled. I was there for a couple weeks, picking coconuts, surfing, living the easy life. But then, as my trip was coming towards the end, I realised that I felt a calling to get outside of my comfort zone. I figured I could probably hitchhike around Maui. I started, still in relaxation mode, getting up past noon so time was already not on my side. I was hitchhiking and I was picked up by all these random people. A stripper, who was also a wedding photographer had a pink dog called Princess Pretty. Hawaii can be a weird place. I made some progress and met some great people as I travelled around the island. I also knew there was a national park/desert lava trail.

When I was close to doing the full circle of the island, there was an area where there were no roads. When I arrived, I was walking and skateboarding until I got to the lava trail. The sun was setting and I started to think about what I was actually doing there. I think most of us have experienced that uncertainty. It got darker, and I saw a grave site for a surfer who had died there, and things looked really gloomy. I was on my own walking and it was getting dark. I had limited food and water because I hadn't expected to take so long. Suddenly, I've been walking for hours and I couldn't see anything except cliffs and rocks. Luckily it was a full moon and so I could see a little bit, but I knew I couldn't continue because it was dangerous. I became exhausted.

Finally, I found some fishermen and I knew I had to ask them for assistance. I asked them how to get to Hana, a city there. They told me I was crazy for trying to get there. They pointed me a road that was 8km away. I was getting cold, I was on my own, and my phone was running out of battery. I put on some music to try and lift my spirits. I knew I'd placed myself in this situation, but it was too late to turn back.

I moved towards this road, and I began having some hallucinations; I thought I could see lights and hear cars because I was exhausted. Finally I saw some houses with lights on near the road, and there was a car. I ran towards it but it didn't stop for me. I didn't know what to do. I decided to go to the house. Obviously, I was exhausted and out of resources. Twenty years old and on the opposite side of the world on an adventure, and it was going completely wrong. I was pretty scared about approaching the houses. I almost walked into a huge cow standing in the road!

I was in the United States, and my mind was thinking about gun laws and the fact that it was midnight. What would people think? I was dirty. But I knew my survival depended on it. I couldn't sleep outside as I didn't have warm enough clothes. It was 10 degrees Celsius and I was in a t-shirt and shorts. I knocked on a door and a super old lady came out. I was so happy that someone opened the door!

I managed to tell my story to her and she gave me some water and a bit of food. I was hoping to sleep there but the daughter of this woman was going to be very concerned because there was a rapist living down the road. It was insane, like a movie. And so this woman was going to be very concerned about this strange, dirty man in the house with her very old mother. They said I couldn't stay there, but that there was a farm down the road where I could probably stay. As I walked the last few miles to the farm, not a single soul crossed my way. Then I saw some head-lights in the distance. I was blessed to catch the only car! And he actually took me pretty close to my friend's house. My friend was shocked to see the state of me when I finally got back!

Wow! That sounds absolutely terrifying!

Simon Skipper: It was but I didn't regret it as I learned a lot and had a great experience.

Love that attitude! Everything I've seen of you is you getting up to adventures. I'm looking at you now; I have a picture of you in a skate park doing crazy tricks. Is there anything on Earth you are not good at?

Simon Skipper: There are plenty of things. I don't consider myself a good cook. I can improvise something when I do have to, but it doesn't happen often. I appreciate food, but I don't need to be the one making it. I'm also bad at drawing, that's why I do photography, I guess.

Don't you think that with anything artistic, we should enjoy it first of all for ourselves, and then for the world?

Simon Skipper: Yes! There's a book I read, I can't remember where I got it, but it says that if you ask in the first grade "Who is great at singing? Who loves to sing?" everyone raises their hand because kids love to sing. But if you ask them five or six years later; because of teen insecurity and comparison, two thirds won't raise their hands. We limit ourselves so much.

That's so true. Kids don't have that inhibition which is conditioned into us. They just do things. We need to find that again.

Simon Skipper: We need to play more. Don't take life so seriously. We're going to be worm food someday, we might as well play around.

What advice would you give to somebody who is an artist in some way, and they're about to enter the real world and make a career from their passion. What advice would you have for them, and also what advice should they ignore?

Simon Skipper: Don't take directions from someone who hasn't been where you're going. This is for everyone, not just artists. That was powerful for me. So many opinions are like a*sholes and everyone has got one. Everyone is busy; family, parents, friends. They're in a different field. People ask if I can make ends meet. I don't need to brag about my financial security, I'm humble. There is an image out there when you're self-employed or freelance. How many people who are in employment are asked if they can make ends meet?

Exactly. There's a stereotype. The "struggling artist." It doesn't have to be like that.

Simon Skipper: No, it doesn't. Be cautious of who you listen to. Park the rest to the side. People are well meaning and trying to be helpful, but they might cause more harm. The advice I would give is to get out there. Don't be a perfectionist about what you're dealing with. Get it out there and fail in things that matter to you. Don't pursue failure but accept it as a learning experience. People like the Beatles and Walt Disney got so many rejections; 40, 50, 60, but look where they are now.

Another piece of advice I would give is that while it's one thing to have a passion for art; I want to honour anyone who has a creative outlet because this is one of life's beauties; when we allow ourselves to be artistic. But at the same time, I want to emphasise that in a capitalistic world you have to focus on creating value and you might have to make compromises. It can be difficult if you only want to only do one specific type of art and you're not offering your skills and talent to help people create value. There are a lot of artists out there who are stubborn.

As a photographer, I'm blessed to fall in love with a craft that is versatile. I can do commissions or do my own work. Find utility for the things you're doing and learn to think as an entrepreneur. If there's an aspect of your business as a craft that you hate, perhaps you need to spend more time with it. If you still hate it after a while then maybe, in the end, your passion is not supposed to be your career. There are plenty of amazing artists who don't have it as their main source of income. And it doesn't make them less of an artist.

Really good point. Simon. Well, you've been incredible. You've given so much good advice. Where can people find you to discover more about what you do?

Simon Skipper: On Instagram: @officialskippz for my photography, and @simplybe._ for the coaching. My website: skipperphotography.dk.
Facebook and LinkedIn are Simon Skipper Christensen.
I'm always happy to share advice when I have the time.

About Simon Skipper

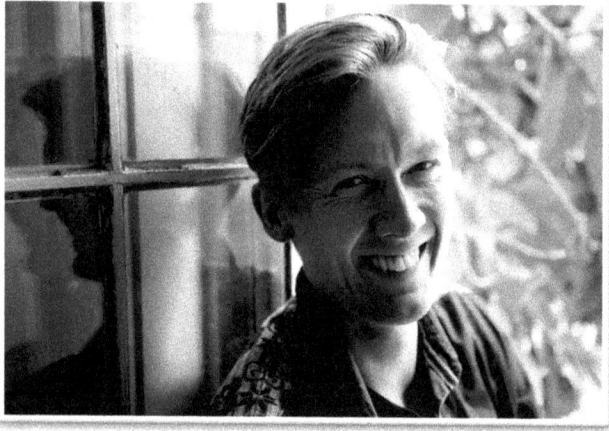

Multi award-winning documentary photographer and CEO of Skipper Photography, Simon Skipper is a sought-after keynote speaker, and coach certified by Emographics/ Tony Robbins Mastery University. A successful entrepreneur and seasoned world traveller, Simon is now helping people visualise their dreams in his capacity as a transformational photographer.

Pairing coaching skills gained through his own personal development with his mastery behind a camera, Simon photographs a vision of his clients that embodies them as the person they are capable of becoming.

Simon has captured images that range from the refugee crisis to astronauts, to the Queen of Denmark on her 75th birthday. During his 10-year career as a successful entrepreneur, he has also co-authored several books in the bestselling Startup Guide series and has been featured on stage and in an array of podcasts and articles.

The transformational photography package that Simon has created teaches his clients how to embrace their vulnerability and be courageous in their lives, whilst always keeping in line with their integrity. The package is comprised of strategic professional/personal coaching sessions and a photoshoot tailored exactly to the needs of you and your business, to create and tell the best possible story; one to make you truly stand out.

WEBSITE
www.SkipperPhotography.dk/about

EMAIL
simon@skipperphotography.dk

LOCATION
Denmark

FACEBOOK
Facebook.com/SimonSkippZ

INSTAGRAM
https://www.instagram.com/p/Byr3I2vhY0s/

How to Effectively Promote Yourself on Facebook

Richard Fletcher is the creator of *The Ecosystem: 42 Days to $100k* – a program designed to transform the business of coaches who are struggling to make money, equipping them with the confidence and the knowledge to stand out as being unique in their field no matter how crowded the market.

Richard learned the hard way that Get Rich Quick doesn't work. He also wants people to understand that this doesn't mean coaches have to get rich slow.

The Ecosystem is a simple method of getting a regular flow of clients without throwing away thousands of dollars in ads. The system can be used on any social media platform. Richard's preferred platform is Facebook, and that is what he is here today to discuss.

Conversation with Richard Fletcher

It's really awesome to talk to you, and what timing! I woke up this morning and you're everywhere. Everybody is talking about your Ecosystem.

Richard Fletcher: I know; all these posts in the US on ABC and Fox, etc. A part of me wondered, "Why do they want to talk about little old me?" But now I'm like, "Yep, I'm awesome!"

The main thing that caught my eye was that you helped a photographer who was charging $1.5k per day immediately change that to $15k, is that right?

Richard Fletcher: Yes. This photographer is in New Zealand and he specialises in what's called "pre-wedding shoots" which I'd never heard of before I spoke to him. But, he's a new Japanese New Zealander, and his market is rich Asians, people from China, Japan and South Korea. They do 'destination' weddings where they fly out and spend a crazy amount of money.

Usually, they look to see who is the most expensive, because they assume they're the best. They fly out six months before the wedding, hire a dress etc., shoot the photos, and go back home. Then, they come back again for the wedding, or may even go somewhere else entirely for the wedding.

For example, they will fly out to Queenstown in New Zealand, go up in a helicopter and get photos on a mountain in the dress and then get married back home. I asked him, "Who's charging the most for what doing what you are doing in Queenstown?" He told me about someone who is charging $10k.

When I asked what services they provided, he told me that it wasn't anything different than what he does. What about the cheapest? "About $500," he told me. When I asked him what the cheapest photographers provide, he said about the same, but without the helicopter and so on. It seemed to me that everyone is providing the same thing, but it all comes down to perception.

Obviously, if your pictures are terrible, or if you're taking them on an iPhone, people are going to notice. But once you know what you're doing with a camera, they do all sort of look the same. There is a subsection of the market, a small percentage of people who are looking for the Valentino and Gucci products. They actively look for the highest-end purchase in this category. To them, it's not only a sign of quality, but also a status symbol. As in: "I'm able to afford $15k per day for a photographer, because I'm rich and successful."

They don't want to pay $1.5k because their friends will look down on them. "You went for this cheap guy, why did you do that?" I said to him, "You're freezing out the low end of people who want to pay $500, and you're also freezing out the high end people who to pay the max." Who's going for the middle guy? I told him I had a strategy, but it's kind of a ballsy move. Was he ready to be brave? "Okay, go on then. What is it?" he said, somewhat reluctantly. "Change your website so that it says "I am the most the expensive wedding photographer in Queenstown, New Zealand... And there's a good reason for that."

Then, we explained why he is the most expensive and the best by showing them pictures of happy couples who are just like your prospective customers. And guess what? Six months later, he's fully booked. He has "too much business" and they're all paying $15k, so he's raising his prices again.

How incredible. He has "the most expensive" on his website, so he's straight out there with it. A really important lesson about perception.

Richard Fletcher: It is. It's about knowing your target market; who you're talking to, and instead of feeling like you're going to alienate the people who can't afford it, you tell yourself that's the point. The majority of people who go to his website will know that they can't afford that rate, but a small percentage who visit will think okay, I'm listening. They start scrolling through the site. His photos are incredible, he's really, really good.

He also made an impressive video. His work is good, obviously you can't do this if you're an amateur, but his work stands up to the statement that he is the most expensive. You look at it, and you know it's really good. But if he only charged $1k, you would think he's not really all that good. That's just how people are. When you're talking about something that is an obvious commodity, a Mars bar for example, where everyone pays 50p and then somebody is charging £10 for it, that doesn't make sense. But when you're talking about a service, perception is everything.

I wouldn't have thought about that with the pricing, but I'm glad that you said you have to make sure you can substantiate your claims.

Richard Fletcher: Exactly. It doesn't necessarily work across all industries. You can't go from charging $1k per month for coaching, then suddenly decide to start charging $100k. There has to be something that justifies that cost. As long as you can justify it, there will be someone who will pay that amount.

The problem is, if you're a brand new coach who has only completed a 2-hour digital marketing coach training the previous weekend, and you don't know anything else, people are going quickly find out. Once they've paid $100k and you don't know what you're talking about when it comes to making them money, they'll look at that.

Business coaching is one of those industries where people expect to get a return on their investment; they want to be able to see whether it's working or not. Whereas, with photography, as long as you provide decent photos, you've done your job.

How did you gain all of this knowledge? What's your background, and what lead you up to this point?

Richard Fletcher: I've done a lot of stuff over the years. I started in 2003 with Herbalife MLM, which didn't work out.

I bought about $3k worth of stock because my upline distributor sold me on the idea that if I wanted to be on the super duper diamond level distributor/coolest guy in the world plan, I had to get more stock up front. She told me that if I was taking my business seriously, I had to sign up to the Max Plan. "Yeah, I'm taking it seriously," I said, like the naive fool I was.

I filled my parents' garage with about $3k worth of stock that never got sold. That was my starting point in business, and it wasn't great.

Then I found another MLM; similar results. I would come home from work and do thirty cold calls every evening from 6 until 8pm. I was ringing a list of people who had been in MLMs before, interrupting them as they were having their dinner. "Who is this? How did you get my number?" they wanted to know. That was soul-destroying. In the three months I spent cold calling, I got one person to sign up.

Sounds awful. What kept you going?

Richard Fletcher: When I speak to people today and they're struggling with their sales calls, I can tell them that I know what it's like as I went through the same feeling back in the day. And I know what needs to be fixed. Sometimes, it's a matter of fixing something specific, and sometimes it's just a case of sticking with it. I then started setting up businesses.

I started my first website, TheTravelMonkey.net, in 2005. It was a site aimed at backpackers, telling them how to travel the world, where to go, how to book cheap tickets, that sort of thing. It did okay considering I had no idea what I was doing.

I built this site, and within a couple of months it had 1.5k unique visitors per month, which isn't loads but it was okay at the time. I received messages telling me that the site was brilliant and thanking me for all the help, but I had no idea how to monetize it.

After six months, I gave it up. Looking back, I realize that I missed out. It could have been a sort of Trip Advisor. I then did a bunch of other stuff; BulkUpFast.com. By the way, if anyone wants to look up these sites, you can go to the internet website archive and see what these sites looked like back in the day, see how far I've come.

Then, I wrote an eBook about online dating. I paid a copywriter about £5k to write a sales web page for me. It was good, but I had no idea how to drive traffic to the site, so that bombed. I just assumed that I'd throw a page up and people would buy it. But nobody's going to buy it if they don't see it, are they?

Do you ever look back at some of the decisions you've made and think how did I not see this?

Richard Fletcher: All the time. How was I such a moron? How did I not connect the dots? This was only in 2010, so not that long ago. This was all while I was doing a day job.

In 2014, I got into dating coaching. I found an online coach who told me to create a program, get people online, take them through the program and charge a bit more for it, rather than trying to sell cheap eBooks. So that's what I did. It took me a while to figure out, including four different rebrands of my website, until I finally hit on something called The No Game Principle.

I won't go into massive detail, but there are a lot of guys who've found all this 'pick up' stuff. A lot of it is sleazy stuff like running routines, memorised lines that they recited to pick up girls in bars. Many of them got caught up in all of that and didn't get great results. To those guys, the idea that you could "be natural," not have to try, not have to remember anything, and having girls like you as a result was really appealing.

Within a week of rebranding my site, I had sold some-one into a new £5k programme, and I signed up more after that. I carried on doing that until last year, when I got married and got sick of talking about dating, and girls, and going to bars. I was speaking to the same guys about the same problems and I lost interest in it. Without mean-ing to, I fell into business coaching and here I am today.

Well, having personally worked with you, I'm very glad that you did. What's the first thing people need to know about organic marketing?

Richard Fletcher: In case anyone is unclear, "organic" is basically anything you don't pay for. Whenever you post on your personal profile, that's organic, you don't pay for it. When you see posts on your Newsfeed that say "sponsored," that's an advert, people are paying for you to see it. I post to my personal profile and not my business page. The reason for this is that your 'reach' – how many people see your post – is much bigger on your personal profile than on your business page. This is because Facebook only shows your post to around 1% of the peo-ple who follow your business page, at present. So, if you have 1k followers, only ten people see that post. It's a complete waste of time. But on your personal profile, a lot more people see it, and you get a lot more interaction.

I've found that people interact much more with personal profiles than they do with business pages. When you see a business post appear, you automatically know that it's come from a business and are much more likely to dismiss it – because you think, "Oh, they are trying to sell me something." You're much more likely to create connections and relationships with a profile post.

Is that allowed on Facebook? Are you allowed to promote your business on your personal profile?

Richard Fletcher: That's a great question, and the answer is no. You have to be really careful about how you promote. When you promote, you're not going in with the hard sell. You know, "Sign up now, doors close at midnight tonight." You can't do that because people will quickly get sick of that and report your profile.

That does happen; it's happened to a few people. Instead, I use more of a soft sell approach. I use posts that get people to engage with me, which gives me likes and comments. This acts as social proof. "Well, other people are listening to this person, they must be worth listening to." I also use what I call 'value posts' that share knowledge that your audience doesn't already know.

A lot of people are making a mistake with their content in that they're trying get people onto their coaching offers, but they're not giving people anything new. "Be authentic." "Show gratitude." "You have to squeeze your gratitude rock at least once a day." When you see posts like this on your feed, you ignore them. It's not that we disagree with the sentiment, it's just obvious. Everyone knows it already. I mean, nobody is sitting there thinking I had no idea, I thought I was supposed to be as fake as humanly possible.

The second piece of advice I offer is that you're not trying to hard sell, but you need to be sure you're actually giving value in your value posts.

For example, you could tell people that you're aware that others in the business are telling them they need authenticity and gratitude, and whilst that's true, simply knowing that isn't going to give them the results they want. You then teach them how they can actually know they're being authentic, what authenticity looks like.

We've all got different facets to our personalities. I've got a side that's quite shy, and I also have a side that's really confident and loud. There's my jokey side, but also my thoughtful side. Which side is me? Which is the authentic side and which is the fake in any given moment? Which side do I decide to share? These are questions that I've never seen answered on Facebook. When you can answer those in a post, then you've offered something of value.

I see a lot of people offering high level suggestions on my feed, the stuff that everyone on the planet knows, but there's rarely a person giving the level of detail that makes it clear that they have a real deep level of insight in their industry, beyond everybody else. When I see someone who is offering that, now I'm paying attention. Now I'm interacting with their posts and I want to see more. When their post appears, I'm paying attention because I know I'm getting value from them.

Yes, that makes perfect sense.

Richard Fletcher: Have you ever read the book *The Seven Habits of Highly Effective People*?

That's one of the first books I read when I started getting into personal development. It basically says that you have to make deposits into the emotional bank account before you take it out. If the bank account is empty, but you're trying to make a withdrawal, you can't do it.

That's the equivalent of a person posting every single day, saying "Join my MLM," but not providing any value. Eventually, you get tire of it. You feel as though this person wants to take from you but doesn't want to give anything in return. But if you give a lot of value up front, if you help them see why what they're doing isn't working, then you're making a deposit in their emotional bank account.

You can ask them for something at a later date, and they won't be so annoyed. They already like you – so they won't report you because they enjoy and appreciate your content.

Another great type of post is what I call a credibility post where you talk about case studies. For example, I might say, "This is how my client went from struggling to enroll people in her program, to signing up three people in one week." I then explain how that happened. I might share a video testimonial; I might tell a story. I might even share a text post as the image. If you share enough of those, maybe around one a week is good, then people can see that you are not full of nonsense.

People can see that you're not full of nonsense, that you do know what you're talking about. One of my best lead-generating posts was about six months ago. It was a live Facebook video. "Here's the three things I did that gave me my first $20k week, and how you can steal this for yourself." Rather than telling people that I was so great because I just had a $20k week, which is more self-serving than anything else, I did it as a value post where I gave them some tips on how to achieve that for themselves.

But what I was really saying was, "I made 20k last week, and you didn't. You need to listen to me, because I know what I'm doing." People listen to that because they can see I get the results for myself, and also other people.

If you're a coach or consultant, for example, a Facebook ads consultant, how can you demonstrate that you're getting results for your clients? Instead of saying "Value post. Value post. Value post," or sticking up some engagement posts, how can you show real results? Because ultimately, I think as consumers, we've never been more skeptical as a society. Would you agree with that?

Richard Fletcher: I don't think I've signed up a single person to a course who hasn't already done at least one course before, sometimes multiple courses, and they've paid at least $10k a pop, but come out feeling disappointed because they haven't received what they felt was value for money. That makes my job harder. When they see me at first, they're coming to me as cynics, and I have to show them I'm getting results. I have to show them that although there are people who have had no results from past courses, they signed up with me and I got them the results they were looking for. It helps people relate if they know there are others who have had the same experience as them. People who have been through programmes and not gotten the result they wanted are actually my target market. These are people who are willing to spend money, because they've done it before, but they're more skeptical than everyone else because they've been burned in the past.

It is a bit of a double-edged sword. They will spend the money, but it's harder to convince them to spend it. But, once you get these people on side, once you get the result for them, they become your lifelong disciples. They love you for it because you helped them when nobody else could.

Wow, that must be an amazing feeling. So going back to posting on Facebook- how often should people post? And are there set times that work best?

Richard Fletcher: I recommend no more than one per day. There are exceptions, but if you are going to post twice in a day, do one at 9am and another at 8pm to spread it out. That way, people in different time zones might see your post. I'll see people post seven times a day, and there's just no way that your audience will see all of them, unless they are your die-hard fans, and so your posts start competing with each other on the Newsfeed. Facebook decides whether or not it will show your post by first showing it to a subsection of your friends. If it gets a decent amount of interaction, then it shows that post to more people. With that in mind, if you post five times a day, your most popular post will be shown to your audience, and the rest disappear into the abyss. It's kind of a waste of time.

Quality over quantity?

Richard Fletcher: Absolutely. Even if you made five amazing posts, only the most popular one would be shown, the rest will disappear. You've kind of wasted time with the other four. Why not spread them out and post one a day, Monday to Friday? There's all your content for the week sorted. I've never seen an example of someone posting multiple times a day while keeping the quality of their posts consistency high. This is a more subtle issue. People seem to think that the more they post, the more people will see it. They want more people to see their posts, so they post as much as possible. But there is a four letter word that we give to the information we receive that we don't welcome or want. Do you know that word?

Spam?

Richard Fletcher: Spam, yes! If you've got someone on your friend list that makes a good post, you think oh, that's interesting, but if they make seven posts in the next day that are all mediocre, suddenly you're not so sure. If they then post another seven more mediocre posts the following day, you might unfollow them, you might even unfriend them. Or, you might just stop reacting to their posts, and Facebook stops showing you their content because it thinks you're not interested.

Because Facebook is always deciding "which of this person's friend's content do I want to show her?" Let's say you're married. If you tell Facebook you're married, it will show your husband's post first because it assumes you're interested in what your husband has to say. Granted, that's an incorrect assumption for many people – but you get the point!

If you're best friends with someone and you always comment on their posts, you comment back and forth all the time, Facebook is going to show you more of their posts. If you talk to someone a lot on Messenger, it will show you their posts because you talk to them and Facebook knows you're friends with each other.

All these little things tie into whether or not someone sees your posts. The more someone interacts with you, the better. If you show them more content, the less likely they are to interact with it. I want to train my audience that every time they see my name in their Newsfeed, that it's going to be something good, something that will benefit them. Something that they're going have a good laugh with, or that they're going to learn from, as opposed to a rambling, nonsense post.

I want to train my audience to think, "The second I see a post from Richard, I need to read every single word of it." My focus is on keeping the quality high. I don't post every day, especially if I'm on holiday. I was away in September, and I think I only posted once that week. I wanted to enjoy my holiday and not talk about business, and I just didn't have much to say, so I didn't say anything. Guess what? My audience didn't forget I existed. They didn't tell me that because they hadn't heard from me in a week, they didn't want to hear from me anymore. It just doesn't work that way. The sky isn't going to fall in if you take a week off; people aren't going to go crazy. I'd rather you waited a couple of days if you don't have a quality post. Because most people are so anxious to keep up the consistency of content, they just put out any old boring rubbish. Are you excited when you've got a load of mediocre content in your Newsfeed? No, you're not.

So how do you turn those engagements into leads?

Richard Fletcher: People have to understand the difference between a post that gets engagement and a post that gets leads. There is some overlap, but generally they are two different things. An engagement post, for example, asks a question that your audience then interacts with. I find inspiration in my daily life that I know will make for good content. A month ago, I was unsure whether to keep eggs in a fridge, so I asked on Facebook. That post got about 100 comments, varying from "in" or "out", to more detailed responses. The way I phrased the question made it as easy as possible for people to interact, particularly if they were replying on their phones.

A good tactic is to stay away from asking common questions we see all the time. "What is your biggest business challenge?" is a question that is asked by so many coaches at the moment, and so it's no longer fresh. By standing out and asking something they likely haven't come across recently (or possibly ever before), they become more willing to interact. In turn, this tells Facebook that people are interested in the post, and that makes it more visible to a wider audience. You're essentially using engagement posts to get yourself onto other people's radars.

Credibility posts are the ones most likely to convert into leads. By sharing a client's journey, you make them relatable to the audience. They could be in a similar place or have similar experiences up to the point that they took you on as their coach/mentor, and this makes it very easy for the audience to picture themselves going through the same process. You're giving proof that your method works.

How do you bring new people in so that they see your content?

Richard Fletcher: I join groups that relate to my target audience, and then interact with their posts and comments or add them as a friend. They then start to see my content on their Newsfeeds and become aware of the advice and help I give. I've had lots of people then contact me on Messenger, telling me that they saw how I helped a person in a comments thread or watched a credibility post, could I do the same for them? That message can quickly turn into a sales conversation.

My main goal is to then quickly whittle down those leads by assessing their financial position and commitment. I also judge whether or not I feel able to work with them on a personal level. It isn't possible to get on with everyone, and I do not want to spend my time with someone I don't enjoy being around. That's not why I left a boring corporate job. There are people who are impolite or abrupt, and they make demands without any common courtesy. Their first message just says, "Tell me about the Ecosystem." They don't say hello or introduce themselves; they just go straight in with a direct order, and I don't have any time for that type of person. It becomes much easier to focus my attention on the leads that I feel have the strongest chance of converting to a sale.

What are the practices to avoid on Facebook?

Richard Fletcher: Well, why are people on Facebook?

They want entertainment. They're looking for social interaction and connection.

Richard Fletcher: They do want that, but the primary motivator behind logging in is boredom. We've reached a point where we can't even bear to sit at a traffic light for thirty seconds without doing something and so we hop on Facebook for a quick look.

Often, it's completely mindless. We suddenly realise we've been scrolling, but not know how we got there.

Richard Fletcher: Exactly. Facebook is designed to give us a dopamine hit whenever we see that little red notification circle. We immediately want to check out who's interacted with our content or profile. It's clever, but dangerous. We scroll our feeds mindlessly because we want to alleviate our boredom. We're not there to learn anything. We don't scroll for knowledge; we scroll for cat videos. Some of us even look for opportunities to be enraged. My programme also teaches people how to be entertaining, but it's not about telling jokes or being a clown. Those that take this approach can come across as insincere, or incredibly awkward. I guide people, using real world examples, on what to avoid. People are seeing so much content that tries too hard to be funny or does nothing more than repeat things they've already heard many times before, and they switch off.

If you've heard it over and over again, it just goes over your head.

Richard Fletcher: It does. Another thing I've come across is a lot of coaches who just aren't good enough at what they do. I've signed up a lot of service providers over the years, and I can probably count on one hand the number of people who are good. Not even brilliant, just good. They see people who are making money online, and they decide to try and get that for themselves. They are not making any money, their health is not in decent shape, and they have no relationship to speak of – yet they decide to call themselves a life coach. These are the people who need to do work on themselves so that they have the level of insight needed to help other people. If you've done nothing more than attend a business course last week in online marketing, you are not able to give any value to the people you're asking money from. Go away and improve yourself, then you can start having credibility. Look at this, you've got me ranting! I wasn't angry until I came on.

And now you're angry. I love it! Any last words of advice?

Richard Fletcher: If you haven't already, just start. Start now. Tell people who you are and what you're doing within your profile and send friend requests to your target audience. Join groups and enter conversations. Create content that is engaging and makes you stand out in this crowded marketplace. Have unique content that adds value to the lives of your audience.

How can people find you out there?

Richard Fletcher: I'm on Facebook (Richard Fletcher), and my website is MagicSauceMarketing.com.

I also have a Facebook group, The Magic Sauce for Online Marketing.

About Richard Fletcher

Richard Fletcher is an upbeat, down-to-earth coach who helps people make more money without spending a lot of money. When Richard claims to make his clients richer, he isn't joking or talking about small sums here and there. It's not unusual for Richard's clients to make between 10K and 20K in a couple of weeks by implementing Richard's tailored plans and advice.

However, Richard's favourite success story is the wedding photographer that was able to up their prices from £1500 to £15000 within one day – and get clients happy to pay a premium for their services.

The driving force of Richard's desire to make money without working too hard is sheer laziness plus of a love of interacting with all types of people. Richard loves to spend time with his wife and cats, and prior to his life as a coach, has been a professional gambler, a dating coach, and a volunteer in a pet rescue centre. However, when Richard finally found his niche, his earnings exploded in a short space of time.

WEBSITE
www.MagicSauceMarketing.com

EMAIL
richard@MagicSauceMarketing.com

LOCATION
England, UK

FACEBOOK
Richard Graham Fletcher

INSTAGRAM
Magic Sauce Marketing

Access Your King's Energy

Henry Johnstone battled severe mental health issues as a young man, and now dedicates his life to helping men to overcome their own mental health challenges. He's a passionate advocate for mental health treatment and recovery for men and heads up a team of coaches that specialise in turning men's lives around.

In this chapter, he shares how you can access your king's energy, what obstacles can come up that may try to prevent you from harnessing this energy, and how you can overcome those to be able to lead your tribe with grace, integrity and confidence.

Henry specialises in working with men, but this chapter is also applicable to women who want to step into the energy of their queen or goddess. The technique works equally well for both men and women.

Conversation with Henry Johnstone

With me today, I have, advocate for men's mental health, Henry Johnstone, and he's with us today to talk about how to access your king's, or indeed your queen's energy. Welcome, Henry.

Henry Johnstone: What an amazing honour to be here with you today.

Your message is incredibly powerful and so needed at this time. What exactly is the King or Queen energy, and how will learning to access that energy benefit the readers?

Henry Johnstone: The best way to frame this is to think of what people perceive the king to be. Anyone reading, I want you to think of the tyrant. You've got a tyrant who lives in a really big castle, he or she is very mistrusting of other people. You probably think they're quiet, insecure, wouldn't let anybody in. He is very, very defensive, keeps everything by his throne, and he's a bit of a mardy bum. And if you're not British, a 'mardy bum' is someone who's a bit grumpy.

And then you think of the king. You know the king lives in exactly the same castle. He's well defended. You walk in, you're happy there because you know the space is taken care of and you know that the king is honorable, he is righteous and he has a safe place to be. You are happy to be ruled by him because he is congruent, he is honorable and he's a good leader. That is the king energy and it is uniquely an adult energy. The tyrant energy is very childish, and the king energy is you, complete as an adult.

And the great thing about the king's energy is that nothing is a risk to the king, because he knows himself so completely that he can be his absolute authentic self in any situation, and they will always be celebrated.

They are cherished, they are celebrated, they are respected. Without question.

What a great explanation! So, you specialise in working with men and talk a lot about the King's energy, but this works for women too, right?

Henry Johnstone: Yes, absolutely. I do have some female clients and what I tend to do is ask them, "Which one sounds best to you? Is it the queen or is it the goddess?" And they choose which resonates with them the most. They mean the same thing—someone who is congruent within themselves and who people will follow, people will respect, people will cherish, and people will celebrate.

I love that you're making sure they're seen as somebody who is worth following. So this isn't about somebody commanding people to do as they say, to lead people into chaos and rule with fear. This is somebody with strong values, who's doing good in the world.

Henry Johnstone: Yes. And the people will willingly follow because they are good people. The King and Queen are good and they are confident. It's almost about charisma.

Let me ask you this. Are you more likely to happily follow someone who speaks to you, if they're not charismatic - you know they're questioning themselves, if you can feel that they're not quite comfortable in their own skin?

No, it's the energy, isn't it? When somebody is really sure of themselves, really confident, I'm drawn to that energy. I want to be around that person.

Henry Johnstone: Yes, because it gives you a safe place to be and express.

Something that I do; I'm very in touch with my king energy. I'm very comfortable with talking about my emotions and being vulnerable. And vulnerability is key to unlocking the king or the queen energy because if you want to do it, you have to be incredibly comfortable with things that have posed a risk to you in the past. You have to be.

I was at a very corporate meeting the other day. I was out of my comfort zone and I thought, *I'm going to step into my king energy*. I'm going to honor myself as I am in this moment.

They said, "Hey Henry, how're you doing?"

I replied, "You know what? I'm feeling quite vulnerable at the moment. This is really out of my comfort zone, but I'm okay. How are you feeling?" And it just blindsided them. They had probably never heard that before in their life, in the corporate environment. But immediately after that, people were drawn to me because I presented myself as a man who wasn't afraid, who was more in touch on a deeper level and it wasn't a risk to me.

So, their vulnerability wasn't a risk to me. They could be vulnerable. I held that space for them to be more of themselves and to be seen.

You seem to have this skill of being able to make people feel comfortable and encouraging them to open up. We were having a conversation about something completely different last week, and the next thing I know, I'm blurting everything out that had been on my mind, and I'm like, 'Oh, what's going on here? Ah, it's Henry just working his magic.'

Henry Johnstone: That is it in its essence. People will feel comfortable around and they'll feel held and there will be no risk. That is the king or the queen in a castle, welcoming people in.

I think that when people think of kings and queens, they may have this misconception that they're always switched on, that there's never anything wrong with them, that they've got everything together all of the time, and that's just not true. Is it?

Henry Johnstone: No, it's not. The strength of the king is knowing that he needs help and being able to ask for help. He has his community around him and he knows that to be a better leader, he needs to invite his tribe to help him, and that's okay.

That takes a level of vulnerability because you're in a place of leadership. You're expecting people to follow you. So it's not intuitive to go, "Do you know what? I'm struggling with this particular aspect of where we're going. I recognize that you are the best person to help me with this. Will you come on board and help me?"

And that's the best thing to do. People go, "Oh my God, I've been seen by my leader. I've been recognized by my leader. He's just told me that he is missing a part in his leadership skill that I can fill'. That's a powerful thing to experience.

So true. A king has a team – he doesn't run the entire kingdom alone!

Henry Johnstone: No

So, you turned your life around from near death to committing to your life's purpose. What can you tell us about that?

Henry Johnstone: Wow! Okay. I lost everything by the choices that I made. I'm a big believer that no one has the power to make us feel anything, no one has the power to make us choose anything. And I really came to a point where I'd lost everything. My health, my state of mind, my family, my friends, my job, any money that was coming in, and I just had to take extreme ownership. If I made these choices, I made this happen. What can I do? No matter how big the mountain of recovery seems, what can I do to take back control? And that was the first time the king energy came up inside me, because it's that responsibility for my kingdom, for my heart, for my sacred self, to build the magnificent castle which I knew I could, but I just didn't know how.

So I was aware, I took responsibility for aspects of my-self that I knew I could improve. And these were things that I was hiding from myself.

So, fear of rejection for speaking my truth was a big one for me, because as a child, I would speak my truth and be rejected. So fast forward to being an adult, I was afraid to speak my truth for fear of being rejected. What's happening there is that my wounded child, the tyrant, was taking over my adult self. It was overruling the king's energy.

I was willingly letting my seven-year-old self come into a 36-year-old man's body and make all the decisions. And I recognize that.

I totally resonate.

Henry Johnstone: But it happens and we're not aware of it because we think we're coming from 'I'm hurt. So, I'm going to go on the defensive,' but it's not. It's your wounded child inside you taking control and dictating how things go. And it is a case of enough is enough.

A child needs direction and nurturing and needs to know that he or she is safe and I'll get on to how you access the child part of yourself so you can bring in the king or queen energy. But that's what I did. I just kept on repeating that process. Whatever made me feel uncom-fortable and vulnerable, I did it anyway, knowing full well that whatever happened was the best thing that could possibly happen because I was speaking from a place of truth.

What challenges did you find when you were going through that process?

Henry Johnstone: As every entrepreneur will recognize –self-doubt, feeling like I was an impostor, feeling like no good would ever come from the work that I was doing.

I had a vision of a man who was in touch with his emotions, who spoke his truth, who was confident, who was a sensitive man I wanted to be that guy. And it was holding onto that vision and following it with my truth, which has been the hardest thing to do.

Going into the coaching business, for example; finding the niche. There's a lot of pressure to find the best niche for you. And I jumped in way too soon and I tried to be the coach that I thought everyone else wanted me to be.

So, I was thinking about everyone else. I was taking the pressure off myself and trying to make a decision based on what millions of people wanted me to be. I was inside their heads, which is ridiculous. I'm not god. I simply don't know.

So I was a confidence and performance coach and I was unhappy. It's also filling false dreams, and I felt under pressure to do so. And it wasn't until I had a breakthrough and I was like, 'Do you know what? This isn't working for me.' What is my truth? What am I hiding from myself? It was the fear of failure.

What if I fail? What if my dream doesn't live up to itself? What if it's just built on a foundation of nothingness? What if every empowering thought I've had about myself is wrong and it falls flat on its face? That is the biggest challenge because it is great coming up with an idea. It is great exploring ourselves.

I always say the moment before action is pregnant with possibility because that's when we allow ourselves to dream, 'I could be this, it could be that.' But taking those first steps into actual action is when all of that comes under the question. And that's what happens.

So, it's maintaining the vision, because that's the power. That's where the king's energy sits. It's within— things aren't going well at the moment, but I'm going to hold my course. I am on the right path. I am going to continue building this vision regardless of what it takes.

And you can notice the child coming in there. If you're in this process, I want to give up. It's someone else's fault. I'm not as good as the other person. They'll always be someone better than me. That's the child. That's the child trying to protect you and get you to step back.

So, what can you do in that case?

Henry Johnstone: You look inside and you become very aware of the one emotion that keeps on coming up consistently. Mine was self-doubt. So I sit with that emotion, and then I track it back. When was the first moment I experienced self-doubt?

I can almost guarantee, I was a kid. I was in class. I put up my hand for the first time ever like, 'I know the answer to this,' but I didn't get the answer right. So I put my hand down. Self-doubt. Can I really trust my thoughts when I speak my truth?

So you track it back to that moment where you feel it most intensely, and you write it down. You acknowledge it. You spend a bit of time in meditation and visualization, seeing your childhood self, experiencing the pain that they felt, really feel it, really accept it that it came from you.

And then you visualize your best self, your kind, loving leader. You welcome in the sovereignty, the sacredness of the king or the queen into your visualization, and you talk to both of them.

Now, the child will have something to say and it may well be the child has had something to say to you for a very, very long time, but you haven't been listening.

Let them speak.

Listen to what they needed back then, which you weren't able to give yourself at the time. You let the king speak and hear what he says to the child. You hold them both and welcome them inside you.

So from that experience, and it goes very, very deep, very, very quickly, you will know the emotional needs that you had as this child, and then you'll have the action that you need to take to accept and to love yourself, which is going to heal that.

And then from that, you look to your situation. I feel like this. This is what I need. How can I take action in this moment to meet that emotional need?

For me, it was, 'I'm going to talk about what I really, really want to do for my business. I need to heal the child who was full of self-doubt. I need him to hear that assuredness. I need him to see that I'm taking action on this, and I need to face that fear.'

And that's exactly what I did. And you know what happened? It was celebrated. I was cherished and I was respected.

A lot of people would just block out that self-doubt that keeps coming back.

Henry Johnstone: Well, that's it. People do block it out because it's uncomfortable. But it's uncomfortable because it's coming from a really deep part of yourself which is shouting for you to address it. But we don't know how to address it necessarily. And the steps that I've just spoken you through, that is exactly how you go about addressing it.

Yes, it is based on visualization, but you need to engage a part of your body which is not your head, because if it stays inside our head, we intellectualize everything and it just goes around in an echo chamber.

We need to integrate the body and the feelings. We need to release it, accept it, acknowledge it, take responsibility for it and take action on what we have learned.

How do you integrate the body?

Henry Johnstone: Integrating the body is simply going back to that place and feeling that emotion. And feel the sensation of where it is. Is it heavy? Is it light? Is it warm? Is it cold? Does it have a texture to it? Situate it inside yourself. For example, 'All my self-doubt comes from inside my chest,' and you remain aware of that.

So, each time it comes up, I put my hand on my chest and I acknowledge it and I take responsibility for it. I created this to protect me from feeling rejected. Am I going to let myself be rejected? No. How do I do that? I speak my truth and I believe in myself and I stand by my word, and when I need to, I speak up and I say it. That is me leading myself in personal leadership.

What if readers do the exercise you just described but they're struggling to pinpoint what that moment was?

Henry: That's absolutely fine. It does happen. It's not always immediate.

I think what happens when people go into the state of, 'I can't think of it, I can't think of it. Oh my god.' You're right back in the head again. Your head has taken over and that's not where you want to be. So it's okay if you can't think of the moment, but you want the feeling that remains the most consistent.

It actually helps to give a scan of the 192 emotions that exist. Do a Google search to find a more expanded language to describe what you might be feeling.

So it might be pensiveness. And if it's not quite pensiveness, what is it? Is it rejection? Is it fair judgment? Is there a little bit of excitement there?

The emotions are incredibly nuanced. Get down to the emotion which is the strongest, and that's where you start. You say, okay. In this exercise, I'm dealing with pensiveness. I created this pensiveness. I don't know where it came from, but I know that it's there and I know that it's intruding on my life, and it is now. That is my child. I'm going to welcome in the king who is going to heal that part within this dialogue that happens in a reflective space. From that, I'm going to take action, which gives me something that I need. Whatever it is that you need to meet that emotional need, feeling pensive.

Maybe you need certainty. Find it and you'll know what it is because you've been resisting going there for fear that you'll always feel rejected and you'll go back to feeling pensive. Does that make sense?

Makes perfect sense!

Henry Johnstone: Good.

Well, that was pure gold; something that anyone reading can go and start doing today, and it can be incredibly powerful. I've heard about your metal retreats; do you use these techniques as part of those?

Henry Johnstone: Yes, metal work really helps people engage with the king inside them, and step into the king energy and to use that to enter into a workshop and create art, which means you have to take responsibility, you have to be aware of your emotions and you have to be able to talk about your emotions all the way through the process.

Tell us more about your metal work retreats.

Henry Johnstone: It's the only one of its kind in the world, and I created the King's Forge Metal Work Retreats because metalwork saved my life. I was rubbish at everything, and I failed consistently. I had all these emotions blocked up. My child-self was in full control. My king was nowhere to be seen.

So, when I got in a metal workshop, and I picked up a welder and I joined steel to steel, I was good at that.

I could do that and it was different, it was cool, and it was a bit dangerous, and I could take responsibility for this piece of equipment which no one else was doing. And it really centered me in an empowered space.

And there's something about creativity that takes the intangible and makes it tangible. So, if you're depressed and you're holding yourself out with some self-limiting beliefs, you can go in the workshop and just be aware of that. And as you work with steel, as the steel changes, your emotional state changes as well.

It's like all these emotions are tied up into a ball and they're all confusing. You don't know which is which. But as you work with the steel, it loosens. People can come into the workshop and say, "I feel I'm a bit afraid, I'm really anxious," "I'm rubbish," or "I can't do any of this". That's all just B.S. They can do it. But they just need the time and the space to explore that.

And that's what happens in the workshop, and it's magic, it is absolute magic. The transformation occurs in a few hours because they can be released. I was struggling to find where that point that the fear of being rejected was, but now I know. It came to me whilst I worked with the steel. Now I know what it is. Now I know what emotional need I have that was being unmet. Now I know how to heal the child and my king is telling me that I can do that, that I can take action, that I can do this thing that I'd been resisting.

I've resisted standing up and doing a presentation for fear that I was going to be rejected. But now I know that it was my child that was afraid. My king won't let that happen. My king has me. My king emerged in the steel, in the fire, in the spots.

Absolutely brilliant. I want to say thank you for coming and sharing so much value today.

Henry Johnstone: Thank you.

Where can our readers find out more about you and your work?

Henry Johnstone: Visit my website at www.KingsForge.co.uk.

Catch me on Facebook, at Facebook.com/groups/mantoman/

And, of course, listen to my podcast here: https://innerwarrior.podbean.com/

About Henry Johnstone

78% of people that take their own lives are male, and men of all ages and backgrounds are suffering from mental distress. On average, one in eight men are diagnosed with a common mental health issue such as anxiety or depression, but it is believed that the real figure is much higher, due to men's reluctance to seek help for mental health issues. How can we help men to deal with their mental health challenges?

Author and men's coach Henry Johnstone spends his life empowering men to tackle their own mental health challenges and discover tactics and solutions. With his groundbreaking Metal Work Retreats, Kingsforge, he has created a structured environment where men learn practical skills that unleash their creativity while teaching them how to manage challenging behaviours, low self-esteem and negative thought patterns, and the value of collaboration and male bonding.

His Mental Health Empowerment podcast challenges the stigma surrounding men's mental health issues, and he has founded a Facebook group, Men Helping Men, which is a growing resource that supports men from all backgrounds.

Many listeners of the podcast are men suffering from undiagnosed mental health issues. Encouraging men to take control of their mental health, as well as reminding them that they're not alone, it is possible to improve the lives of these listeners, and aid them in seeking help for depression, anxiety and suicidal ideation. These resources are also valuable to the parents and partners of boys and men with mental health issues.

Henry is also co-writing a book with his father on the subject of mental illness and adversity.

JOHN MARSHALL

How to Create a Framework for Success as a Small Business Owner

Most business owners know their business is capable of more. More revenue, more profit, more growth, more free time, but they're stuck. John Marshall of Results Driven calls it being stuck on the entrepreneur treadmill. They want to get off and stay off, but they can't do it on their own.

That's why John created Results Driven – a five-part framework developed to help entrepreneurs finally achieve the results they deserve. The outcome for entrepreneurs is having more confidence in their abilities so they feel empowered to take control of their future. They start to see tangible benefits like increased profit, increased revenue, and increased overall ability because they're being transformed into a better version of themselves. They're starting to see what they're capable of doing. John has worked with clients in more than 30 different industries over the last 15 years and has given them all a framework to follow to create success.

Conversation with John Marshall

What is the results driven framework based on?

John Marshall: The framework is based on five key areas necessary for business growth. The first is an innovative tool called "What's your number." This allows the business owner to score the health of their business on a scale of 1 to 100. Suddenly, they learn how healthy, unhealthy or underperforming their businesses is on a scale of 1 to 100 based on six key areas. Once they complete this quiz and get their score, they know what areas need improvement.

The second part of the framework is helping them create a strategic commitment plan which has three parts. The strategy part is what they need to do for the next three years. It forces them to examine their core value proposition, their core uniqueness, and core ideal customers. The next part is the commitment part of the plan which is what they need to do for the next year. This includes identifying their goals, measurable goals, what their marketing plan is, what kind of scorecard they need to create, what obstacles they're going to face in the year, etc. A third element of the plan is identifying what their number one goal is, and what's needed to meet that goal in the next 60 or 90 days.

Then the next part of the framework includes success strategies, or continuing education. There are 12 strategies, so they're always learning, growing and developing which is what highly successful entrepreneurs want and need. It's what keeps the stickiness or the glue in the results-driven framework and includes ongoing coaching and mentoring. Every two to three weeks, I sit down with my clients and have a one-on-one scheduled phone call for 45 minutes to an hour that is focused on them and their business and what is needed to be done together based on their plan to help them get greater results.

Can you describe the difference you see your program is making in the lives of those you help?

John Marshall: The difference is dramatic. It's significant because they're suddenly seeing what their business is finally capable of and what they're finally capable of. They are getting the help that they need from a proven system. I started to see over time their increased confidence which is a critical component to business growth. They now know what they need to start doing, stop doing, and continuing doing to be successful. They've got a plan. They've taken the movie that's in their head, that plays literally every day and through the day, and put it on paper. They've documented the steps and I help them to work on that plan step by step. So, they take the right steps in the right order to get the right results.

What myths or misconceptions do your clients have before working with you?

John Marshall: It's always one of two things. Many times, they've had a bad experience with a consultant or consulting firm or a business coach. Often, it's because many people label themselves as a coach and frankly, they are not qualified to be that. They try to do their best, but they don't have the skills, the experience, the wisdom, or the processes to really help. So, if anybody's ever previously had a coach and hasn't had results, it's because they have chosen the wrong coach. So that's a fear.

The other fear I see is in their decision to get started with Results Driven. As soon as they do get started; however, they say one of two things. Number one, I wish I'd started sooner because I'm getting terrific results. Or two, I wish I'd heard of you sooner because I really needed help on my business and now, you're delivering on that. Part of our philosophy at Results Driven is to be visible, to get ourselves aligned with the business owners in all these different industries that need help and say, wow, there's something out there called Results Driven. I want to be part of this because I want success and I want somebody to help me step by step to get there.

How do you help them overcome misconceptions and fears?

John Marshall: Business owners will often hire us because they've been thinking about getting help for the last six or nine months and they'll say, you know, I'm looking for some advice. They will usually come with their own preconceived notions from books they may have read, podcasts they've listened to, YouTube videos watched, etc. But what they want now is somebody to help them with their specific business challenges, locally, one-on-one. They have the mindset of, you know, I'm ready for this. If they're not quite ready or seem hesitant, I'll have a conversation with them on the phone or in-person and run some numbers, do a return on investment analysis and see if it would be a good fit.

It's important that I know what they are trying to accomplish and what their motivation level is before accepting them as a client because my objective from day one is to make sure that we drive enough new revenue and more importantly, profits back into their business so the investment in the program is at least cost-neutral, or better yet, a three times, four times, five times 10 times return. I've had many clients follow up with me, one as recently as two weeks ago, "John, I can't believe how beneficial this has been. I've paid for your services in increased profit for the next 10 years. That's how helpful you've been to myself and my team and my business."

What are the biggest mistakes you see business owners and entrepreneurs making?

John Marshall: I think the biggest mistake is they don't have clarity on how they help their target market. I do a tremendous amount of networking and I ask people I meet what they do. It surprises me how many can't articulate what they do in benefit-driven language. When I ask them to share more details or give me more information while I'm standing in front of them and having a conversation, they still don't understand what they do. If they don't understand what they do, I can't help them. They can't help their clients.

The second part is that they do not have clarity, but more importantly, they're not working with their core customers because they don't know who their core customers are. They haven't identified that they spend a tremendous amount of time, energy, focus and money not getting the great results they should because they're wasting time in the wrong market and they can't provide a clear solution on how they can help. As a result, they spin their wheels and I call it being trapped on the entrepreneur treadmill.

I sit down with them and get really clear on their business model. They need to know specifics on how they help their clients. We also help them with their vision. What their business can look like a year from now, three years from now, but the biggest help is finally creating a plan, a system, a process so they can create success in the future with a definitive plan one step at a time. If they struggle in developing their plan, which is often quite common, that's where we help. We help them to create that plan.

Here's the secret sauce. They have to implement the plan even if they don't continue to work with us or it's just a short-term project. The disconnect for them and the reason they don't get success is they don't implement their plan. They don't have accountability and as a result, they just flail away and hope that they're going to be successful.

The secret sauce or the secret formula is the continuous implementation by taking action, by having us work with them on a regular basis, every couple of weeks, or a minimum once a month which keeps them on track. They course correct and they are accountable for their actions because we're having that conversation consistently and regularly about what they're doing, what they're not doing, and what's going to move the needle in a positive direction in their business.

What's your inspiration for doing what you do?

John Marshall: I worked for Proctor and Gamble at a university. I was the only one selected that year and had a great time, but I suddenly realized I'm not a corporate guy. My inspiration to start my own company began with a conversation I had with a prospective client. I was in Denver at the time and working as a sales and marketing director for a home care company. I rang up this woman, and the conversation went like this. "Hi, I'm in home care. You're in home care. Would it make sense for us to have a meeting and maybe we can share leads, you know, create some joint venture opportunities"? She said, okay.

I met her at her office, and we started to talk about how we could work together in homecare, the firm I'd worked for as well as her own firm, and I thought, wow, this is a really good niche. She seems very interested, so at the end of the meeting, I felt like we were going to work together, and I asked her "So does that sound good to you"? And she said to me, "I've got to tell you I'm not interested. I'm not interested whatsoever."

I went, wow. In my head I thought, okay, I guess I didn't read that particular opportunity very well. She said, "John, what I'm more interested in is hiring you as my marketing director." And I said, geez I'm really flattered, but there must be some miscommunication. I didn't come looking for a job, I don't have a resume with me. I'm really sorry I miscommunicated. I get ready to leave, and I turned to her and sat back down in the chair in front of her desk and I said, "Can I ask you a question?"

I told her I've always wanted to have my own business mentoring, coaching, consulting company and asked, "Would you consider being my first client?" She said she'd love to. So, I kept my full-time job and I would drive up and work with her every Monday from about six-thirty at night to about eight-thirty at night helping her with sales, marketing, finance, and operations.

She had bought a franchise and she should have been getting help from the franchisor, but she wasn't. And I thought that was not really fair, so I began to work with her one-on-one. I didn't have the tools that I have today at Results Driven and yet, within five or six months, I helped to double her revenue and that's when I knew my calling was to help other small business owners be successful.

About six or nine months after that, we were having a conversation and she started to cry. I said, "Wow, what did I say or do?" She said, "John, I'm not crying for what you said, or what you didn't in today's meeting, I'm crying because had I not met you, I came to the realization, John, I would have gone out of business. I would have lost my investment with the franchise and I'm so thankful that you and I connected because now I have a successful business. These tears are tears of joy." I told her that I'm just thankful to you because I love what I'm doing. I really enjoy helping. And I think it's unfortunate when small businesses are just like you don't get help because you would've gone out of business and that's a shame.

I'm trying to right a wrong and that's what drives me every day. I'm working with clients all across North America now in 30 industries. It's just magnificent that I'm able to help the business owners. I speak at conferences, I get invited to speak at events, at keynotes, and I get to share how we can help. And sometimes these people become clients. I genuinely love what I do because I'm able to give them the specifics, the skills, and the step by step of exactly what they need to be successful.

What do you think is the most important question entrepreneurs should ask themselves before they consider hiring a coach or consultant?

John Marshall: I always recommend asking for a track record of success. Who have you helped and how did you help? It's important to get the specifics from the consultants. Ask the see the materials and any tools that they are going to help you with.

One of the first tools I use when I work with every single client is called "What's your number." I give it to the clients for free. They answer the questions and right away they get a benchmark on how healthy or unhealthy or underperforming their business is in six areas. And the neat thing about that tool is it's their score. It's not me saying, I think you're a 55 out of a hundred or 25 or 95. They self-score.

At that point, if they want to go further with Results Driven, they can. If not, we just stop there and just wait for them to eventually contact us. I would say the question would be, you know, what is your track record? How do you help and what tools do you have to support me and make me successful?

About John Marshall

John Marshall is the founder of Results Driven. He is a thought leader and authority on small business. After graduating from business school, he met entrepreneurs worldwide and discovered something very powerful. Too many entrepreneurs were trapped on the treadmill of day-to-day activities. They struggled because they lacked focus, a defined plan, and the ability to prioritize. They knew deep down their business should be more rewarding.

John knew he could help. Drawing on skills he learned at Procter & Gamble, his business degree, and best practices from consulting in over 30 industries, he developed a 5-part training framework that gets results.

WEBSITE
www.results-driven.com

EMAIL
john@results-driven.com

Key Concepts for Productive & Efficient Meetings

Ruth helps people communicate better. This includes designing better meetings, redesigning business processes, and solving problems and conflicts that arise within organizations. The word facilitate means "to make it easy," and that's why her clients come to her. They have organizational and process issues, or they are experiencing conflict within the organization. They want it to be easier and to move forward. I sit down with Ruth to get an understanding of the importance of facilitation during conflict and how she helps her clients.

Conversation with Ruth Nicholson

What are the biggest problems that trigger the need for facilitation?

Ruth Nicholson: Because we're often working with other people, focus is the biggest problem I see. We're listening to respond, and we're thinking ahead about what we want to say or what our response will be instead of listening. Sometimes what we say and what we intend to say doesn't match up as well as it could.

When we come together in conversation, there's a purpose for that conversation even if we don't actually point to it and can explain it. When I'm helping people create a conversation or create a meeting, I have them fill in the blank of this sentence: *The purpose of this meeting is to...* I want them to finish that sentence because the more clarity people have about what they need to accomplish with a conversation, the easier that conversation is going to be, and the less we are going to wander all over the place. People get frustrated when they're trying to have a conversation and it doesn't feel like they've gotten to the point or it doesn't feel like they have come to a resolution. It doesn't feel like they produced the outcomes they wanted to produce.

How many meetings have you been to where it lasted an hour, maybe two hours, and you think to yourself, we talked a lot but what did we accomplish? If I had to put my work in one word, it would be **focus** because I can help people identify what they want to accomplish, and then we can work together to figure out how to do that.

It sounds simple, but I think people get frustrated in corporate America, in nonprofits, and in government agencies. The statistics on how many hours people spend in meetings and what they think about the productivity of those meetings are really scary. Meetings are often how we get work done. When we have good meetings, the outcome is a better result in less time.

Can you give an example?

Ruth Nicholson: Last fall, I was working with the board of directors of a credit union to develop their annual strategic plan. There were about 15 people in a room, and they came from big, high-powered companies. Both board members and staff were there. We went over all of the numbers, productivity statistics, growth opportunities, and strategic program areas from the past year and how they wanted to work on in their business. We spent the morning sharing all that information through a lot of presentations.

All that was asking the first question about their business: **WHAT?** What is it that we need to know? Then we asked: **SO WHAT?** We looked at what it all meant. What is it we need to understand about all that data, and what does it tell us? What are the implications? What are the trends? Then, we asked the action question: **NOW WHAT?** What are we going to do about it?

We structured this one-day planning meeting around those three very simple questions: What? So what? Now what? We talked through them and got down to the implications, the desires, the hopes, and the dreams so that the credit union could do specific things to achieve its goals in the coming year. The meeting was scheduled to go from 8:00 am until 5:00 pm, but we got out at 2:30 pm. We completed ALL of the work that needed to be done. The board and staff looked at each other, and they said, "We thought we were going to be here until 5:00 or maybe a little later. We accomplished our work and a complete board strategic plan in less than a day!"

The next meeting was developing the implementation plan with the staff. Once again, the all-day meeting was scheduled from 8:00 am until 5:00 pm. Once again, we decreased the meeting time and increased the outcome. We got out at 3:30 pm because we were focused, we had a plan, and we got it done. People looked around and said, "You mean we don't have to be here late?" Not if the work is done! Take it. Run with it. Go be successful.

With focus, you can get more done in a shorter amount of time. Who doesn't want a shorter meeting?

How do you identify the source of conflict?

Ruth Nicholson: We don't always see where conflict is born or the sources of conflict. Each of us wants to think of ourselves as intelligent, capable, and valuable. That's a good thing. When we work in an organization, it's a little bit like being on a sports team. There are all kinds of different positions on a sports team. If you're a soccer player, you have goalkeepers, forwards to score goals, defenders who try to help keep the goals from happening. There are 11 players out there. They each have a different role. If they all play their roles, the team is probably going to be successful. But, if one of the players has the mindset of "My position is the most important of all, they can't live without me, and I should be able to tell everybody how it should be," this attitude creates tension. If I think I'm the most important position, and you think you're the most important position, and so do the other people on the team, we've now created an alpha dog situation.

I may be the goalkeeper, and I may be an expert goalkeeper, but you know what? I may not know a whole lot about actually being a forward and scoring goals. But I know how to stop them! I call this the Alpha Dog Syndrome where the thinking is: I'm the expert, and you should bow down to my expertise.

If you put a bunch of alpha dogs in a room together, you get conflict because each of them thinks they are the only one qualified to lead. Within organizations, it's more like being sled dogs. They're all pulling in the same direction (or at least we hope they are). We might even rotate the lead dog depending on the project we're working on. If we're working on budget kinds of things, hopefully, there are some experts on money and budget we can ask to be the lead on that issue. If we're working on service delivery or customer service, we've got some people who are experts at customer success and customer support, and they can be the leaders when we're working on those things.

It's about honoring the expertise we bring and being humble enough to know that not one of us is good at it at all. It's not always up to the person who's been in the company the longest. It's the mindset that everybody has a superpower and then bringing that to the table with the confidence of the gift you're giving the group and the humility of knowing that other people's gifts need to be factored in. When we're under stress, or when we're in conflict, it's hard to remember to do that because we get in defensive mode, and we listen only to respond instead of listening to understand. We need each other's knowledge. When we're under stress we get threatened and stop listening a lot faster.

What are the common mistakes and pitfalls?

Ruth Nicholson: I once worked for the federal government in a very large organization as the internal facilitator. Any department could call and say, "We're having a meeting. Would you help us out?" I had a team of facilitators that I could deploy to help people facilitate good meetings. The first question I would ask is: "Why do you want a facilitator?" I could always see their brains going, "Wait a minute, I just called the facilitation office. Why on earth would she ask why do you want a facilitator? Of course, I want a facilitator!" The purpose of the question was to identify their expectations for a facilitator.

What do you want the role of a facilitator to be? Do you want a mediator? Because you know there's going to be conflict. Do you want a Master of Ceremonies, an MC? Just somebody to keep time and make people feel good and move the thing along? Do you want somebody to help design a meeting and not just create an agenda but *design* a meeting so the interactions are unique and get the work done? Do you want a note-taker? What is it that you expect out of that person? Sometimes people would call and say, "I want a facilitator," but what they really wanted was somebody to deliver bad news. (Well guess what, that's not what facilitators do.)

Many people don't think consciously of the many roles the facilitator can play. I have a client right now that has a very large board with a six-standing committee. I facilitate all of them. With this particular group, I'm helping them design the meetings, but the chairs of the committees run their meetings. I'm co-facilitating with an elected chair, but I'm not standing up in front of the room leading the meeting. I'm co-facilitating as support to the elected chair. It's still facilitation, but it's more in the design. If things go sideways, I jump in. Knowing what you can expect and knowing what you need is critical. It's back to focus. That's what's going to make a successful outcome.

How do you assess needs, misconceptions, and fears?

Ruth Nicholson: I once taught conflict resolution to third graders at our neighborhood elementary school. I would walk in with an orange and get two children to help me with this skit. I said, "Hey, I've got an orange." The two children would say, "We want the orange!" I turned to the class and I said, "Oops, I only brought one orange, but there are two children that want the orange. What should I do?" The third graders will look at me like, "Well, lady, just cut it in half." But when I tell them I'm going to cut it in half, the two little kids in my skit say, "No! No! No! We don't like that idea. That doesn't work for us."

Now, I turned back to the class and said, "The obvious solution isn't going to work, so what should we do now?" Then I was quiet. We don't like silence. We want to fill the silence. Finally, somebody would say, "Why do they want the orange?" So, I asked the two children. The little girl says, "I am so hungry. I want to eat the orange. I'm very hungry!" Then I turned to the little boy and asked why he wanted the orange. He explains, "It's my mom's birthday, and she loves cake with orange frosting on it. I want the zest of the orange to make my mom's birthday cake."

The point to the little skit is that the nugget mediators bring to the conflict in difficult meetings is the concept of listening to understand and then separating positions from interests. In the orange story, "I want the orange" is the position. Both little kids had the same position, and we had a conflict.

The minute you get curious and you listen to understand and ask what's behind that position is when all of a sudden, your universe of solutions is bigger than just cutting an orange in half. You can find other ways to help meet those interests. Of course, not every conflict we have is as simple as a story about an orange, but you will learn more, and you will discover the possibility of more solutions – and solutions that might even be better – when you ask "Why?", "Tell me more," and "Help me understand why this is important to you."

In my work, I want to fully understand the expectations of what work you want me to do as your facilitator. What do you need out of this meeting or this series of meetings? What does success look like for you? When I first start with a new client, I'm scoping out the job. I determine how much preparation is needed, who's doing the agenda, who's taking the notes, what the roles are around supporting and implementing this meeting or this conversation. Did you know that there are really only three things we do in meetings? One, we share information, or we gather information in meetings. Two, we analyze information. We make sense of it. We look at the trends. We talk about what it means and what the implications are. Three, we make decisions.

How many of us have been to a meeting and somebody brought a flip chart? We spent hours talking, and we filled up all those flip charts with lists and ideas, and at the end of the day, the room is covered in flip charts. We're exhausted. You walk out of the meeting, and I bet you that most of those times, you gathered information, and you might've talked information to death. You might have analyzed it a whole bunch, but if the purpose of that meeting was to make a decision, it's like not finishing a good meal. You didn't achieve the purpose.

People will feel that disconnect where we were supposed to accomplish something, and we did a whole lot of work, and we didn't get finished. We weren't successful. So are you sharing information? Are you analyzing and making sense of information? Or are you making a decision? Meeting success goes right back to the three questions we used in the strategic planning meeting: What? So What? Now What? "What" is about information. "So what" is about making sense and analyzing information. "Now what" is about making decisions.

What is your inspiration for helping organizations with conflict resolution?

Ruth Nicholson: Facilitation is a survival skill in my family that I learned from my mother. When she was alive, for every client engagement or training session I had, she would call me and ask how it went. What she was really asking was our standard for success—if I gave people something in terms of a tool or an approach or a successful meeting that would make their life better tomorrow than it was today. My work is my mother's legacy. And what about tomorrow? Tomorrow is all about my three grandkids, her great-grandchildren. Whether I'm working in nuclear waste cleanup or banking or natural resources or youth sports, I've got three grandkids. A better tomorrow matter to me.

About Ruth Nicholson

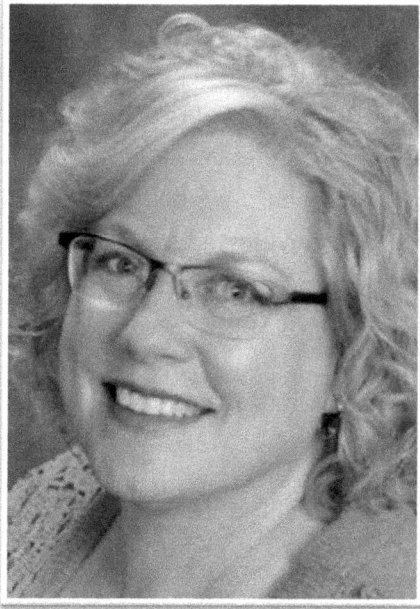

Ruth E. Nicholson, Manager of Nicholson Facilitation & Associates, LLC, is an International Association of Facilitators (IAF) Certified Professional Facilitator (CPF), visual and graphic facilitator, Certified Assessor, and trained mediator in private practice in Snohomish County, Washington USA.

She is also a member of the US Institute for Environmental Conflict Resolution (USIECR) roster. She holds a master's degree in public administration and offers over 20 years' experience in organizational development, facilitation, conflict resolution, public policy, and non-profit organization management.

Ruth has also worked in youth and semi-professional sports, particularly soccer, for more than 30 years. She was one of four national finalists for the 2018 Hudl Innovator of the Year in youth soccer award. She is an avid writer and workshop presenter for youth sports blogs and coaching education events, including national sports leadership events, conferences, and conventions.

Ruth's passion is helping people build the relationships necessary to develop sustainable agreements and build well-functioning organizations.

WEBSITE
www.NicholsonFacilitation.com

EMAIL
Ruth@NicholsonFacilitation.com

How to Maximize Your Potential & Gain Confidence Through Leadership Development & Coaching

Monique works with leaders who want to maximize their leadership potential and impact. She also helps leaders and organizations achieve higher levels of self-awareness, fulfillment, synergy, and performance so they achieve unprecedented results and have a positive impact on the world. Specialties include executive coaching, leadership development, communication, collaboration, team effectiveness, group facilitation, change management (Prosci certified), organizational diagnosis, and conflict management.

In this interview, Monique and discuss how she helps her clients maximize their potential

Conversation with Monique Breault

How do you help your clients get better results with leadership coaching?

Monique Breault: There are two major services that I offer. The first is leadership coaching, and often it's coaching executives. People typically come to me because they are stuck. They're stuck in terms of advancing their career or they're stuck in terms of not feeling like they're having the influence or impact that they would like to have in their work or their lives. Oftentimes, there's a sense of dissatisfaction or frustration. It's a feeling that there's got to be more to life than this. It's an existential question and there is usually some kind of suffering or pain that they are experiencing.

I find that we grow the most when we're going through some kind of crisis in our lives. It can be a relationship at work that's not working or feeling like they're just not achieving everything that they could be in the workplace and they'd like to do more of that. Those are the key problems I help them solve. They want to generate more results, but they're finding that they're not able to do so. Most times, their challenge has to do with owning their impact and creating strong relationships. It also has to do with how they see themselves as a leader.

As a result of working on themselves and who they are as a leader, coaching helps leaders be more effective and have more impact and influence. Developing a really good relationship with their inner leader liberates them to have better relationships with others. My clients also say coaching provides them a greater sense of fulfillment and resilience to navigate the challenges of organizational life.

In part, the reason they achieve this is because they have a broader perspective that's related to critical leadership topics. Everybody's different. There's always going to be a different challenge that is present for people. I help them look at who they are while facing that challenge and then provide them with relevant tools. I help them look at their mindset. How are they looking at the challenge? How are they seeing others, how are they seeing themselves? And then I help them develop new mindsets and new skills, and they experiment to see what works and see what doesn't.

I also help them achieve a clear sense of their vision as a leader and why they are put on the planet. We explore their purpose: the intersection of their unique contribution and what the world needs from them right now. I help them get clear on their values. Vision, purpose, and values are extremely grounding; they help us navigate the challenges that show up in our lives. I also help them achieve self-awareness of their perceived strengths and development areas. Higher-level leaders need to get feedback from a variety of sources. Self-perception is often not accurate, at least in terms of the big picture. Perception is reality and is seen differently by different people and so I make sure to collect data on the leader either through interviews or surveys which reveal strengths and areas to work on.

It also comes down to awareness of their inner resources and roadblocks because that is really what's getting in the way of people achieving their potential. I believe leadership is an inside-out process I have them look at what they have available inside themselves to address whatever challenges are coming up because who we are is how we lead.

As we go through life, we're going to hit ups and downs. It's important to develop resilience. It's about how do I pick myself up off the ground when I've had a tumble, and how do I see the learning in difficult experiences? How do I still honor who I am and see myself as worthy when I've had a challenging time in my life at work or home?

Developing that resilience is possible when a person develops a better relationship with their inner leader which is a combination of three things: self-acceptance, self-compassion, and self-authority. I describe a leader as anyone responsible for their world. There's the word "responsible" meaning responsible for achieving results, managing employees or leading an organization. There's also another way of looking at the word responsible and that's "response-able" which means able to choose how to respond to a situation and instead of a knee jerk or a typical reaction. We all react to stress in different ways; I help people become aware of their reactive habits.

There are usually three types of reactions to challenges or stressful situations. Some people push back and fight. Some withdraw or freeze. Others become duty-oriented, appease and tend and befriend. Once we know what our patterns are, we can look at what's underneath that and then we can create a bigger space between the event that triggers us and our response to that event. I help people create more space so they have the exquisite moment of choice of how to respond. They can choose whether to follow their old habits or try out with different responses that can lead to better results and stronger relationships.

The second service I offer is a teambuilding service. I help teams develop trust, have productive conflict, set goals, be accountable, and achieve results.

What are some common myths and misconceptions you come across while working with clients?

Monique Breault: The biggest myth is that you should only develop high-potential leaders. I see many organizations investing in the coaching and development of their senior executives, and people that are on some kind of a succession path, but they invest less in the people at other levels. Since everyone is a leader, developing everyone's leadership potential – no matter their level – can benefit the organization.

There is also a misconception that only a team in trouble needs attention. A team is a living entity that is continuously changing and going through different stages of development. They have different needs at each of those stages. I see organizations signing up for team building but then not knowing what they want to achieve. Having fun together is important, but it's not just about having fun. A team needs to pay attention to its needs. Sometimes they need to be kicking off in a way and developing trust and relationships. Sometimes they need to work through conflict.

Conflict resolution is the biggest and most important skill teams and leaders need to develop. I was just chatting yesterday with the CEO of a firm that I was brought in to do some conflict resolution because they were not addressing the conflict themselves and it came to a head. Every organization, every relationship is going to have moments when people don't see things the same way, so they need to build their skills and the ability to stay in a tough conversation.

The third misconception is that we are logical beings or "heads on a stick." Society and organizations tend to have us check our emotions at the door when in fact, becoming emotionally intelligent is the best way for us to connect to us ourselves and connect to others. It's not all about logic. Yes, we do have a logical side and it's important to focus on facts and numbers, but it's been proven that humans make decisions based on emotion. So, the more conscious we can become about how we do that, the better decisions we can make.

What prevents organizations from getting a leadership coach?

Monique Breault: Organizations may hesitate because coaching is not cheap. Really good coaching from somebody with experience and who is well certified is not cheap and so they may hesitate to invest. It's been proven time and time again that investing in a leadership coach is one of the best ways to get more productivity, more engagement, and more results. When coaching first started in the 1980s or late 1970s, it was for remedial purposes. The thought was, "We need to bring somebody in to fix something or fix a person." Coaching is not about fixing. It's about accepting what is there and polishing it to bring out that person's strengths. That requires seeing them as creative, healthy and whole while helping them get in touch with their inner wisdom.

I help them understand what coaching is today as opposed to what it used to be. Some clients have come to me and said, "I'm scared because I was assigned a coach. What does that mean? Does it mean that I'm on my way out?" I reassure them that the company is investing in you because they believe in you and they feel that you working with a coach is going to help the bottom line even more. And I made sure to work with Human Resources or whoever is bringing me in and paying the bill to ensure that that's how they view coaching as well. Otherwise, I don't take on an engagement.

It's difficult when organizations believe that performance management is best done by a coach. I find that what they truly need is for people to learn how to better handle conflict and give and receive feedback more often and more effectively. Some coaches specialize in remedial cases. I do not because I believe performance management is the responsibility of the organization.

Can you share some examples?

Monique Breault: Leaders can be afraid of expressing themselves, not feeling fulfilled at work, not being seen and acknowledged. Humans share three basic needs: to feel worthy, to feel loved, and to feel safe. We're socialized to look outside ourselves these things. I help my clients find those things inside instead.

I recently worked with an executive who had a lot of doubt about his impact and influence. He had the habit we all often do of looking outside for answers. He also frequently looked to his manager for acknowledgment or recognition. What helped him the most was letting go of being attached to that. I helped him get in touch with his inner wisdom and navigate those times when he felt fear and anxiety. It's a very common emotion.

I helped him with mindfulness practices. I helped him learn how to stay in difficult conversations with people. I helped him learn how to trust himself and how to take risks without thinking that it's going to be the end of the world. I also helped him look at the negative scenarios that he was spinning up, which a lot of us do, and ask himself, how realistic are they? What are the chances that this bad thing will happen? He would often laugh and say, "You know, pretty minor. I don't think that'll happen." This is a person that has succeeded for a very long time in his life in various environments, but he was new to this organization and he was still kind of finding his sea legs which created a lot of fear and anxiety. People often come to me because they are told that they are having a negative impact on others and as a result, others aren't giving their best work.

Another example is a man that recently contacted me from a very large manufacturing company because he realized that he had more things to learn about how to interact with people to get better results. His communication approach led employees to fear him. People were avoiding him. And it turns out that he was steamrolling people. He had a very high level of power in the organization, but his temper was getting in the way of productivity.

It turns out that he was seeing people as objects and not as human beings. I helped him realize that and what the impact was which opened his eyes. All of a sudden, he started changing how he interacted with people. He would show interest in their lives. He would be more patient with them. He would watch his impulse to jump in and fix things. He became more patient and in touch with his compassionate side and was able to show some vulnerability, which is often why people steamroll others because they don't want to be steamrolled themselves.

The HR manager called me after I worked with him and asked, "What drug are you giving this man? Because he is just a very different person. He is civil. People enjoy working with him now. What's going on?" It was lovely to hear that his practicing new mindsets and behaviors were having a positive impact. This is inspirational for me and why I do what I do.

When I worked for Hewlett Packard back in the late nineties and early 2000 as an organization development consultant, I would work with the general managers and the senior executives helping them run the people side of things in their organization. I've found that the moments that brought me the most flow and the most joy and the places where I noticed the biggest impact were the ones where I was having one-on-one leadership, coaching conversations with people and where I just felt in my gut that this was the work I was meant to do. I could feel a sense of connection with the other person. I got feedback that they were transformed as a result of working with me and they were so much happier.

I then realized, wow, I want to do more of this because it feels like it's my calling and it's something that I'm good at and it's something that impacts people. As I've become more experienced, I've realized that my calling is to grow conscious, connected, compassionate, courageous leaders in service to a whole and healed world because there's a lot of suffering in the world. I work every day towards answering the questions of how we can alleviate that suffering and how can we learn to show up in a way that is more loving and honors the interconnection that we have with one another?

Can you share a lesson learned early on that impacts how you help clients today?

Monique Breault: I learned early on that I need to value the work that I do if people are going to pay for it. I need to ask for what I'm worth. There's a tendency when you open a practice to want clients; I would undervalue what my consulting was worth and that meant that my business didn't grow as fast as it could have or be as profitable as it could have been. I learned to develop confidence in what I offer and ask for what I'm worth. I've also discovered that people will pay more for something if they think it's more worthwhile. It's a really interesting human tendency.

What should organizations consider before working with a leadership coach?

Monique Breault: Before I begin working with a client, I ask them how courageous their leaders are. I think that's the most important question. There is a popular book written by Dr. Brene Brown titled "Dare to Lead" in which Brown interviewed 100 CEOs and asked them, "What do you think is most important right now in the world?" And they said, "Courageous leadership."

Before working with me, I also want them to know how they will measure the success of the coaching intervention and how they will know and track that things have changed. When evaluating and choosing a coach, they need to check out the credentials of the person and their experience, but then give the executives a chance to interview several coaches to establish if there's chemistry or not. Because like any professional relationship, coaching is a very personal one, and to go deep, you have to trust somebody. Some people feel more open with different types of personalities than others, so I think it's always important for people to interview more than one coach to see who fits best and who's going to meet their needs best.

About Monique Breault

Monique Breault helps leaders and teams achieve out-standing results by intentionally envisioning, enacting and evolving their shared future. She has over twenty-five years' experience coaching leaders and teams to perform to their potential and make a lasting impact in their world. Monique brings a partnering mindset, deep, insightful listening, and a creative, holistic approach to every engagement.

Throughout her career, Monique has been fascinated by the tension between our human need for connection and our desire to amplify results through collaboration, which bumps into the fact that we are designed for survival and have emotion-based reactions that make us focus on ourselves. Monique is passionate about cross-cultural communication and how to help teams with diverse members make the most of their differences and achieve synergy.

Monique managed intercultural training programs at Procter & Gamble in Japan and led organizational transformation and leadership development efforts at Hewlett-Packard. Her clients include Nike, Sony, US Cellular, CH2MHill, Genworth, The Port of Portland, The Standard, Social Venture Partners International, Waggener Edstrom, and the Washington Department of Labor & Industry.

In her off time, Monique enjoys hiking, yoga, photography, International films, hanging out with friends and chilling with her husband Carlo and their cats Cammie and Jasper. She also reads. A lot!

WEBSITE
www.MoniqueBreault.com

EMAIL
monique@moniquebreault.com

DEBORA MASTEN

The Importance of Advanced Training for Spa Profitability

Debora Masten is an independent contractor and she operates a wellness center in Oregon offering advanced aesthetic services. As a consultant, she is often called in to help provide training or instruction to new hires in a spa or to train the entire staff on a new modality.

Debora also teaches continuing education at the Academy of Advanced Aesthetics. This includes modalities like micro-needling, IPL, laser and acoustic pressure wave for facial rejuvenation. Her goal is to provide classes that certified advanced aestheticians want to take. She is also often called in by advanced aesthetics schools that need help with program development. Debora is also an independent sales and educational representative for several manufacturers of skincare products and related devices and has been working with AnteAge since 2013.

I sit down with Debora to get a better understanding of how she helps her students and clients.

Conversation with Debora Masten

Why do aestheticians need to increase their knowledge base or start adding more advanced procedures?

Debora Masten: When you've been in the business for a long time, you get some pearls of wisdom along the way. If I have someone that is saying, "Hey, I bought this piece of equipment but I'm not getting the results," we talk about ways to improve the efficacy of the treatments. It often comes down to deductive reasoning skills. I tell my students the sign of a good laser technician or aesthetician is the deductive reasoning skills because not everybody fits in that same box. You really must be able to look at several different areas and decide what direction to go. For example, what and when to start a procedure to get their skin healthy. That's the goal. Sometimes that means no treatment until good skincare is established.

I find that a lot of med spas or aestheticians want to do the treatment first and do the skincare program later. I'm trying to reverse that. I say, "Let's look at your deductive reasoning skills and how you're approaching these devices and how we can maybe make the performance better. It's not just the device, take a good look at what you are doing either pre or post that also influences that treatment."

When you have someone newly licensed, you go through training and you have basic skills. Most people understand you must be a lifelong learner. In this field, things are changing all the time and just because you did things with one device doesn't mean that it's going to work the same with another. If you have used a certain laser before, you can't assume you don't need training on a different one. Just because you've used an 810diode laser for hair removal doesn't mean that a 1064 yag laser is going to respond the same way. Knowledge helps provide safe, consistent, quality services.

Most people are very cautious until they become comfortable with a new device. For example, if they switched from a diode to a YAG, there's a learning curve that can create some problems. For instance, a 1064 yag has limitations for finer hair because of the longer wavelength even with using a short-pulsed width duration. I can help implement solutions. Being able to overcome obstacles and solve problems is part of my assessment.

How do your clients find you?

Debora Masten: They find me either on LinkedIn or through a website I have with the Academy of Advanced Aesthetics. I don't market my consulting business in many places. Many of my consulting clients are referrals from laser repair centers, word of mouth, and from manufacturers. Any interested clients can certainly reach out to me and I'm more than happy to see if I'm a fit for their needs based on what their issues are. I don't claim to be able to help with everything, but I would certainly try to point them in the right direction or find someone else that could. I have had experience in the treatment room, the classroom, with sales and marketing and in quality control and operational procedures including laser safety.

How do you assess their needs?

Debora Masten: It starts with a quick phone conversation to understand what the client is after. I will then do an evaluation which gives me an idea of the possible needs. I look at their overall practice and operations and see what changes can be made and how best to implement them. My goal is to have a clear role in the plan for success and a timeline in which that will happen.

It's about listening to what's happening and understanding why a client is reaching out for help. Sometimes the girls don't know how to sell a product, or they aren't getting the results the client wants. I look at ways (through training) to change that. Once I analyze the situation, I then create a plan to retain and grow their client base and staff. Retention is important in this industry. If you can't keep the clients that you already have, that's a problem and you won't see growth or increased profits. Doing a review of performance helps to be alerted to what is and isn't working.

What are some of the objections spa owners may have before working with you?

Debora Masten: Depending on what their specific problems are, clients need to know that I have the knowledge and credentials to help with that issue. If I am not the one, I will try and find them someone better qualified for their specific needs. Sometimes I will give them free advice if it's a lack of budgeted funds. I've helped many solo practices over my career. Once they see success, they find that my services are worth paying for, so they give me a call.

One thing I tell my clients is that selling products is vital because everybody needs them. Clients are all buying skincare somewhere, right? So set your goal every week. Take a product, for example, a cleanser for all skin types and have everybody mention the cleanser to every client today because everybody washes their face. See how many more cleansers you sell by bringing that small goal to your staff. List successes on a whiteboard for staff to see. What's the product sales for this week? Set mini goals instead of "everyone's got to sell $500.00 worth in this amount of time."

It's much easier to make small goals That is one of the little things that I'll share with them at the beginning. If that doesn't work, then, maybe I'm not the right person for you, but I'll give you some little tips, try this and see if it works. I enjoy those callbacks that say, "We sold 25 cleansers this week and normally we sell three."

Can you give an example of how you helped a client overcome an obstacle?

Debora Masten: One Medi Spa with new employees was unable to use some of the handpieces for their device because they weren't trained. Clients were asking for this treatment, but because no one was trained on the pixel handpiece, no services were being performed and they were losing business. I was able to go in and train the entire staff at one time. We lined up clients that could be used as models, went over potential safety issues and protocols that were associated with using this handpiece and how to get the best results. I also covered some of the best ways to sell this treatment on their menu. The owner was then able to add this into their service menu because the aestheticians were trained, confident, and ready. It's about quality assurance standards and making sure that they're doing everything properly. Sometimes this can be accomplished very quickly depending on the experience levels of the staff.

What inspired you to get into this industry?

Debora Masten: I kind of fell into aesthetics by accident. I was working for a physician at the time doing marketing and consultations for his sclerotherapy business and he wanted to buy a laser for hair removal. I was trained and soon I was running two of his clinics doing laser hair removal and some other procedures. It was at the beginning of the aesthetics boom in 1998. Lasers for hair removal were cutting edge at the time and I found that I just loved it.

I then went to school and I got my aesthetics license while I was working in the medical office. I have worked at Oregon Health Sciences University, worked in laser sales and education for skincare companies as well as running my clinic. I served as the Chairman of Oregon State Board of Cosmetology for two terms and on the Nation Interstate Council skincare liaison committee. I am also a subject matter expert for the State of Oregon Cosmetology board for Laser and Advanced modalities.

Can you share any lessons that you learned early on that still impacts how you operate today?

Debora Masten: The biggest thing for me is that I'm very hands-on. I have adult children and my son always says mom, you could've been franchised. I was one of the first in our area operating a laser hair removal clinic. I'm not a good people manager and I know that about myself. I'm the type that when I'm cooking, instead of having somebody come help me, I just do it myself. I'm very much that kind of a person. I feel like I know how to do it and I do it better. And that's a bad thing. You must trust your employees. If you want to grow, you must hire good people.

I've had to learn I can't be everywhere. You must get good people and trust them. That's a hard thing for me and I had to adjust along the way. I take personal pride in my work, and I feel that way in my consulting business as well. If I don't have the answer, I will find out for you or point you in the right direction.

What should spa owners consider when they're evaluating further education and consulting options?

Debora Masten: It depends on the state in which you live. It's important to know if you can legally perform non-ablative cosmetic procedures. Is it in your scope of practice? Are you working under a physician as a medical assistant? What can basic licensed aestheticians do? What can advance aestheticians do? What can you do under a physician if you're an employee? There's no sense in getting training for something if you're not going to be able to use it in your state. I primarily work in the Northwest, but there have been instances where I've traveled to different places like New Orleans and New York. Know your scope of practice and what training is required to qualify you to add a service or treatment.

Another consideration is how much practical hands-on time is required in addition to theory. You should know what the return on that investment is. Sometimes aestheticians will take training on individual techniques. They'll want to come in for say, micro-needling and have a class. If you need continuing education credits, then you need to seek out those that are going to fit your needs as well as fit your pocketbook. If you're just out of basic facial technology school, then I would suggest making sure that you reinforce your skills. Be proficient and the profits will come.

If you're a spa owner and offering education and training to your staff remember, people are very mobile these days and if you invest too much you may not get a return. Think about servicing, staffing, equipment training, compliance, files and forms, practice guidelines and safety officers. It's important to look deep and evaluate what exactly you want to accomplish and determine if it's going to fit your needs.

Happy clients are a big key because you don't want bad reviews on Yelp or Google or social media. You also don't want clients asking for their money back. Those things are damaging. They hurt you and you must know how to manage all that before it affects your bottom line.

Also know what to give away and what not to give away. I see a lot of spa owners giving away things that cost them money. If you're going to do a promotion, know what that promotion is costing you and know what you are going to get from it. Remember, time is money too. You must track everything.

I still see many day spas relying on daily deals on the hope that they will get loyal clients. Do you typically recommend this approach?

Debora Masten: No, they're usually just looking for something cheap. Occasionally, you'll get a client that may stick around. I say, "Make them not want to go anywhere else." Do all those little things but don't give too much away. Don't be the highest, don't be the lowest, but have your prices high enough that occasionally you can offer a discount. Or perhaps you can offer a special or a yearly program on return service. There are lots of ways to market and discount and compete with daily deal sites, but you must do it creatively and don't give away so much that you're not making anything for your time.

I encourage spas to do offer something that's self-service, like LED lights where the client can lay down and relax. They're going to make money without paying a technician to do those things. That's a way to increase your profit margins. Be sure to communicate that it is a self-service procedure so your client doesn't expect anything different. Give away those kinds of things if you must offer an extremely discounted service.

About Debora Masten

Debora has been a practicing esthetician and laser technician for over 20 years. Her career has included owning her own laser center, teaching esthetics education, working for OHSU, representing and educating for product and laser manufacturers, and serving as a consultant and subject matter expert for the state of Oregon. Debora recently helped many estheticians with the necessary education to obtain their advance esthetics certificates.

WEBSITE
www.salemskincare.com

EMAIL
info@salemskincare.com

Mistakes to Avoid When Getting A First Time Home Loan

Buying a home, especially for the first time, can feel like a daunting process. Finding the right professionals to help you through the process will put your mind at ease and ensure the process is as smooth and stress free as possible. Nicole Tennison is one of those professionals.

I sit down with Nicole to find out how she helps her clients navigate the complexities of the mortgage process.

Conversation with Nicole Tennison

How long does it typically take to close a mortgage for a first home?

Nicole Tennison: We can close in about 20 days. I'm always available to my clients. I can be reached directly on my cell phone, they can text me, send me a video at night or on the weekends. This makes a huge difference because most of my clients are making offers at night or on the weekend. So, they are able to get a preapproval letter or ask questions outside of the nine to five when they are normally working.

I like to make sure my clients understand the full process. I give them all the options so they can make an informed decision on what the right program is for them.

I help them with all of the steps that ensure the process is smooth and without worry. Once they find a house and make an offer, I contact the listing agent on that house to let them know my clients are fully pre-approved for their financing. We can close on time and that gives my client a competitive edge over others making offers on the same house. So, that's something I do that's a little bit different.

I'm a firm believer in educating my clients on all the products available and what goes into the pre-approval process for getting a mortgage. I teach home buyer classes at my office about once a month, sometimes twice a month, and I recommend that those buying or wanting to buy attend that class. The class covers the entire home buying process over the long programs and goes in-depth about credit.

Most people don't know about the credit process. They're scared about running their credit, they're scared they're not going to qualify. There's a lot of fear of the unknown. So, by taking the class, they learn exactly what is involved, and knowledge is power. They feel empowered after they leave.

If buyers are unavailable to take the class, I'll go over the buying process with them separately. At that time, we will review their credit and talk about the next steps. I then present all of the options available to them so they can make an educated decision. Once we get someone pre-approved, I'll talk with their real estate agent because it's a team effort.

What are the common myths and misconceptions you encounter?

Nicole Tennison: Many people believe they need a large down payment to purchase a home—as much as 20% down. However, there are down payment assistance programs that allow some buyers to get into a home with as little as $500 out of pocket. I'll have people come to me when they are referred by a friend and they'll say, "Oh, , I don't think I'm going to qualify. I don't have a down payment." I tell them that we offer down payment assistance and they have never heard of that before.

Another misconception that buyers have is their credit score isn't high enough. Clients will tell me, "Oh, my credit is not good enough. I have a 650 credit score" To qualify a buyer, we need a 620 or higher credit score.

Many of my clients are surprised that they don't need a large down payment or they already have good enough credit.

Sometimes people think it's easier to go with an online lender. It's really not. You still have to complete their application and submit your documents. We have an app called "The Fairway Now App" that allows you to complete an application in about 10 minutes. All required documents can be uploaded through the app. We're just as easy to work with as some of the online lenders that claim to have one click and you're done process.

I recommend prospective buyers have all of their documents reviewed upfront, including their income review and their credit reports, so their financing does not fall through.

Unfortunately, I've had folks come to me who have been pre-qualified online by other banks that didn't really look at their full income documentation and other qualifying factors that all lenders use. This can result in a denial a week before they're supposed to close on their new house. Sometimes I can help them, but it depends on the reason why they were denied. That's why I tell my clients it's better to get everything done upfront and have your income documents submitted and reviewed to decrease the chance of your financing falling through at the end.

Another potentially costly mistake to avoid is making big purchases before closing. I've seen buyers purchase a car within a couple of months of closing and that can really damage someone's credit, especially if they use the dealership's financing because the dealership tends to pull credit multiple times. Credit scores can drop a 100 to

150 points. I recommend that they don't buy any vehicles or use their credit card. Also, do not open a card at a department store and use all the available credit – this will drop your credit score.

I explain the importance of not making purchases until after closing to my clients so they get pre-approved. If they take my home buyer class, we go over what to do and what not to do. They may not realize that buying a car can really hurt their credit or that using their credit cards can also negatively affect their credit. I'm a firm believer educating buyers on the process and how important credit is.

Case in point: I have a client right now who was referred to me and his credit for a VA financing was about 80 points lower than where he needed to be. I used a tool called a "credit simulator" that will tell me what can be done to increase someone's score. I then wrote out a plan for him that included specific steps such as pay this down, write a letter here to get that dropped, etc. so he could improve his credit score. A couple of months later, he got his credit to where it needed to be and now, he's in contract and we'll be closing on his VA purchase next week.

What lessons have you learned in the many years you have been in this business?

Nicole Tennison: I grew up around the business. My mother was a commercial loan officer and my grandmother was a banker. When I got a little bit older, I would sometimes go to a closing with my mom and I really enjoyed it. I really enjoy people. I guess you could say I'm a people person. I did dabble a bit in the commercial world, but I really wanted to help first-time home buyers. That is my passion and that's what I love doing because of all the emotions involved and helping someone achieve their dream. There's a lot of fear and excitement. It's the biggest investment for most people, it's the biggest purchase that they will make in their life, and it's also the biggest asset that they have in their lives.

Homeownership is still the number one way Americans build wealth, so for me, just helping someone through the process, educating them, going through all those emotions and getting them their keys in hand is very gratifying. It's why I get up every morning and do what I do. I love taking them through that process and getting homeowners into their first property. I've helped a lot of my clients move up from the first to second to a third home. I'm just really grateful to be a part of that process and helping them achieve their financial future and building their home and their families. So that's, that's my inspiration

When I first started in this business, I didn't know as much about credit or what documents I needed to review fully upfront. Occasionally, I would miss something, and it would complicate the process at the end. I've learned to review all of the documents and do my due diligence upfront and let my clients know to get everything reviewed in the very beginning so I can ensure the loan will close on time.

Do you have any recommendations before working with a mortgage broker?

Nicole Tennison: I recommend carefully vetting a Mortgage Broker. Does this person have experience? I have learned a lot through experience. A seasoned loan officer is going to know more about specific programs and offer you more options than someone who is new to the industry and may not know all of the options available.

It's also important to ask, am I comfortable with this person? You want to make sure you're comfortable and this is someone who is easy to work with because through the process, you're going to be talking quite often and you're going to be pretty close to them until you find a home. I've had clients come to me and not buy for years. You need to know that they're giving you the best options and that they're, putting your best interests first.

Do they offer all the programs that I am looking for? Not everyone offers down payment assistance or certain other programs so be sure to ask if they are available. Many offers are made in the evenings and on the weekends and it can be frustrating as a buyer if you find your dream home on a Sunday and you need to get that pre-approval letter to make sure that your offer is accepted, so that's definitely something I would ask.

About Nicole Tennison

Nicole Tennison has been a Mortgage Broker specializing in first-time home buying since 2002. She helps her clients get on a plan to do all the things required for a smooth approval process, including raising credit scores if necessary. In certain cases, they might meet the minimum qualifications for credit, but if they paid off a debt or contest an item on the report, it often ends up raising their credit score and enables them to secure better terms on their loan.

Most other banks and lenders do not offer this service. Nicole takes pride in giving extra value to her clients resulting in a quick closing that improves the chances of an offer being accepted. She believes trust and honesty are the most important qualities to look for in a mortgage lender.

WEBSITE

NicoleTennison.com

EMAIL

Nicole.tennison@fairwaymc.com

LOCATION

Lynwood, WA

www.ingramcontent.com/pod-product-compliance
Lightning Source LLC
Chambersburg PA
CBHW062023200326
41519CB00017B/4897